PERSPECTIVES ON

CONGREGATIONAL LEADERSHIP

*Applying systems thinking
for effective leadership*

ISRAEL GALINDO

Perspectives on Congregational Leadership
Copyright © 2009, Israel Galindo
All rights reserved.

ISBN 978-09715765-7-5

ACKNOWLEDGEMENTS:
"The Myth of Competence," originally published in *Congregations* magazine, Alban Institute (Winter 2003); "Ministry Years" appeared as "Staying Put," originally published in *Congregations* magazine, Alban Institute (Winter 2004).' "Systems Preaching" appeared as "What's Systems Got to do With It?" in *Congregations*, Alban Institute (Spring 2007). "Leading from the Right Side of the Brain," appeared in the Leadership in Ministry Workshops newsletter Vol. 7 No. 2 (Summer 2007).

Published by Educational Consultants
www.israelgalindo.com

CONTENTS

III. CONGREGATIONS AND ORGANIZATIONS

Bibliography

Introduction

The intriguing concept "positive deviance" refers to the phenomenon that, all things being equal, certain individuals in any system are able to function at a higher level than others, and thereby, are a positive influence on the system. Why is it, for example, that one pastor is able to succeed in a particular congregation, while another, in a similar, or the same congregation, fails? Why do some congregations thrive while others do not, even when they share the same denominational affiliation, geographical location, resources, and demographic? For sociologists, one answer to those questions is the identification of a positive deviant in the system, a person whose capacity to think, and function, differently than others in the system brings about healthy change.

Bowen Family Systems Theory (BFST) continues to grow in its influence among clergy, denominational leaders, and seminaries. I think this is a good thing, overall. Many have found in BFST a frame of reference that helps them develop into positive deviants in their congregational systems. The theory enables them to understand the nature of congregations, leadership, and relationships more accurately than a "devotional" or metaphorical mindset does. Theological and biblical metaphors have their place—but they fall short in accurately explaining what it is that actually is going on in the messy and complex dynamics of human emotional systems.

At times BFST suffers the plight of all things that move from obscurity to popularity: misunderstanding, misapplication, overuse, oversimplification, and an unwarranted assumption that "being familiar" with the theory is equivalent to actually understanding it. Further, similar to all things that contain esoteric knowledge and have as their goal self-understanding, there is that tendency to confuse comprehending intellectual concepts with *apprehending* truth and insight at the level to which it belongs: the intuitive and affective. And, further, there is the misguided notion that understanding something is the same as actually doing it.

One interesting phenomenon I've witnessed is how initial interest in BFST tends to fade quickly when the pragmatist's question is raised. It's a question I hear often in my philosophy course.

Student: "This is all really interesting, Dr. G., but what am I supposed to do with this?"

Dr. G: "Well, you don't actually *do* anything with this. It's not that kind of knowledge."

Student: "O.K., but how is learning this going to help me in my ministry?"

Dr. G: "Ummm, it probably won't help you at all in your ministry. It's not that kind of learning."

Student: "O.K. Whatever. Do I still have time to drop this course?"

Over the years I've seen a long trail of eager visitors to the Leadership in Ministry Workshops come and check it out only to check out very quickly. They tend not to find the answers they are looking for—namely, answers to the question of how to get people to do what they want, or, how to "fix" their congregations. If certain folks find BFST "useless" it may be because it seems to lack the pragmatic quick fix so many are looking for—a modern day penchant among leaders that Edwin H. Friedman wrote about at length in his book, *A Failure of Nerve: Leadership in the Age of the Quick Fix*.[1]

The reason BFST may seem useless to the pragmatic-minded is that, like philosophy, it's not a "tool" that one uses to fix, adjust, change, or mold others. It does not provide gnostic "power" from a source of secret knowledge. Nor does it bestow abilities, skills, or techniques that guarantee mastery over others, a stay against bad situations or the fates. Neither does it relieve self-doubt, personal insecurities or cover a multitude of personal flaws and deficits.

Some enter into the study of Bowen Family Systems Theory out of curiosity. These are the seekers, students, and those fascinated by "systems" of all kinds (MBTI, Enneagram, etc.). Some are drawn to the promise of discovering another leadership secret that will help them be more effective, or at least, appear to be. And others come because they are hurt, numb, or desperate after being pummeled in particularly toxic ministry settings. For those who are able to give up those initial motivations and stick with the program the next stage often is just acquiring a functional understanding of the terms, concepts, and theory. After that there are varying ways to work at applying the theory. But that, again, is not a matter of mastering techniques. Applying the theory has to do with working on one's own internal emotional self: working on family of origin issues, working at one's emotional and relational functioning, and taking more responsibility for one's well-being, goals, values, and emotional health. Those who stick with it are the ones who have come to appreciate that there's no quick fix when it comes to being an effective leader. This is what we call "life work," and it takes a long time—the rest of your life.

For those who are not able to commit to that life work, and would rather acquire tricks and techniques to make their life and work "easier," BFST will remain just another interesting field of study. The danger is achieving expertise without change and knowledge without wisdom.

This book is a collection of "deviant perspectives" on congregational leadership based on concepts in Bowen Family Systems theory. That is, these perspectives tend to fall outside the normative thinking about leadership in congregations. What I've observed in those who commit to the hard work of growth and personal change is that at some point or another they have changed their perspectives about themselves and leadership, and, emerge as the positive deviants in their systems, whether a congregation or a family.

[1]Edwin H. Friedman, *A Failure of Nerve: Leadership in the Age of the Quick Fix* (New York: Seabury Books, 2007).

I. THE FUNDAMENTALS

Is BFST a Valid Theory?

A friend asked where Bowen Family Systems Theory (BFST) fell in the divide between subjective and objective. "In other words," he asked, "is it a valid theory?" It was an interesting question that led to some stimulating conversation. Since the ideas in this book are grounded in BFST, it is worth exploring the question as to the soundness of their foundation.

Personally, I would put BFST more on the subjective-interpretive side. While some proponents of BFST claim it to be "scientific," it is not so, technically speaking, nor in the sense of traditional "scientific inquiry method." The "science" that it depends on is from the "soft" sciences: clinical psychology, psychotherapy, sociology, anthropology, etc. The claim that the theory is grounded in the "biological" sciences must be tempered by the fact that while it tries to stay close to the "observable facts" of living systems it must yet make some imaginative interpretive leaps at points. This is not to denigrate it, nor to discount its validity; all theories of necessity must do so—even "scientific" ones. With BFST we're dealing with one additional wild card: human beings who have free will, have the capacity for being self-determinative, have the capacity to will, and whose life circumstances have too many variables to anticipate or fit much into a category of "normative." If there's one thing we can say for certain about human individuals and the systems in which they exist, it is that they will always surprise you no matter how many "rules" or "principles" you come up with to explain their behavior and motives. Such is the reality of "emotional process" and human relationships.

Here are the things I think make a theory "valid":

- It describes reality as it is perceived
- It is internally consistent
- It is comprehensive: explains all phenomenon in its area of focus and concern
- It is universally applicable to all objects of its concern (to all organic systems, to all relationship systems, etc.)
- It is disprovable (it is honest, based on observable facts, and not akin to "magical thinking" or an ideology).

Given that list as criteria, BFST is a valid theory. I don't think there's a need to make it "more scientific" than it is to give it validity.

How to Learn Leadership

I received an e-mail from a friend who has been studying Bowen Family Systems Theory (BFST) for the past few years. He has been reading the literature, asking good questions, and at one point sought out a therapist to serve as a "systems coach." In his email he expressed desire to continue studying, and his question hinted that he had hit a plateau in his learning to become a more effective leader—not uncommon in any learning enterprise.

He asked, "I was wondering if you could recommend any other ways of learning better about Bowen theory and leadership, short of doing an actual training program."

I didn't have any new ideas for my friend. It seemed to me that he was doing the work that was necessary. There is no magic bullet for learning BFST, or for becoming an effective leader, other than persistence. Ultimately, being a student of leadership is not about knowing more. It's not about mastery of concepts (although that is important) and it's not about acquiring more knowledge (although that's always a helpful thing). Ultimately, it's about working on one's personal growth in order to bring about change in one's emotional growth. That's a different kind of learning and it requires a different epistemology—more self-understanding than "book learning."

Though there is no one best way to learn the theory, there are certain things one can do to learn more. Taken together they work if we commit to doing these things on an on-going basis. Here are the things that seem to work:

Reading and studying the literature. Understanding the concepts and principles of leadership theory is important. At the very least it helps us avoid misunderstanding. The more we read the more we move from naïve to sophisticated understanding. I've found that it is helpful to read both popular and academic sources, theoretical and practical, and clinical and interpretive. Reading the literature is not so much about learning the answers as much as it is about learning to ask different questions and gaining wisdom from others' experiences.

Working on your family of origin. I am convinced that there is no better "lab" for learning the theory and about ourselves as leaders than our own families. That's because to really "get" emotional process we must experience it, and that's what our families allow. If you really want to change your emotional functioning, then work on your relationships in your family of origin. If you really want to understand the theory, then work on your genogram.

Working with a coach or a coaching group. Working with a coach or coaching group provides the resource of perspective. No matter how learned we are in the theory, it remains difficult to see emotional process within ourselves and within the systems we are a part of. Coaches help provide perspective, interpretation, reminders, and challenge. This practice is an indispensable resource to learning and living the theory.

Attend the occasional workshop or seminar. Hearing how other people apply or interpret the theory is always enlightening. For those who find reading a challenge because of their learning styles, listening to others unpack the theory can be a very helpful pathway to understanding. Even listening to a taped audio or video presentation can help.

Write about it. One of the most helpful pathways to insight is writing. Writing can pull together hunches, fuzzy thoughts, inklings, and muddled ideas into a coherent thought. Whether it's writing about an idea or concept, or, writing about one's experience, putting pencil to paper (or, tapping it out on the computer keyboard) helps sharpen our thinking and often teases out an insight.

There is no magic pill or shortcut for the things that have the most potential to bring about fundamental and long-term change. It's a matter of persistence, hard work, and intentionality. It also requires the courage to be open to being challenged and changed.

Misunderstandings

Few things escape the consequences of their own success. This axiom seems true even of Bowen Family Systems Theory. It seems that systems theory is now the "in" thing—never have there been as many courses on it, or more "experts" on the matter. And a sure sign of its popularity is the rate of books being turned out that claim to have a "systems approach to" something or other (this book being one of them!). This is, overall, a good thing. The more the theory is propagated, the better, I say. But one consequence of the theory's fast dissemination is the risk of misunderstandings—like in that old parlor game, "telegraph." What goes in one ear at one end may come out as something completely different at the other—the message gets lost in translation as it is passed from one person to another.

I continue to hear many "misunderstandings" related to Bowen Family Systems Theory (BFST) and its application to leadership. And while I'm no self-appointed guardian of the truth, I am enough of an advocate for critical thinking—and admittedly have little patience for "fuzzy thinking"—that I often find myself offering correctives when I hear a misapplication or misunderstanding of the theory. After all, both, I think, can have dire consequences. Below, then, are correctives to some of the more common "systems misunderstandings."

Systems theory is about leadership. The fact is that BFST is primarily about therapy. But the theory identifies principles about relationships and relationship systems that are universally applicable to any context in which people form attachments or live and work together. The application of this theory to the concerns of leadership is appropriate. But to believe that systems theory is a "style of leadership" is a fundamental misunderstanding.

Systems theory is about managing conflict. For those unfortunate enough to occupy a leadership position, this is the cold hard truth: conflict exists and it cannot be managed. To assume that systems theory provides a way to manage other people's behaviors, emotions, beliefs, or anxiety is a fundamental error. What system theory offers the leader is a way to manage him or herself amid the conflict that arises as a natural course of events in any relationship system.

Systems theory is about managing change. Sorry, it's not about this either. How do you "manage" the nature of the cosmos? Change, in both evolution and entropy, is the nature of the world we live in. The typical misunderstanding here is that systems theory is a tool to use in managing other people, relationships, organizations, and circumstance. Holding on to that misunderstanding will do a leader in every time. If systems theory is about anything, it is about managing self in the midst of the constant changes around us.

Busyness is the same as overfunctioning. The complexity of congregational ministry means that pastoral leaders will always be busy. In fact, the longer one stays in one context, assuming the leader is working at organizational development and institutional evolution, the more complex the ministry becomes, and, the busier the job. Overfunctioning involves taking responsibility for things that are not yours to take on: other people's jobs, anxieties, or responsibilities. Effective leaders are busy about the things for which they are responsible—and they will always be busy. The point is to avoid overfunctioning—being busy because you are doing other people's jobs, or worse, perpetuating patterns of overfunctioning-underfunctioning reciprocity.

Self-definition is the same as Self-differentiation. Self-definition is merely the act of stating what you believe about yourself or about an issue. While that is important, it is not equivalent to self-differentiation, which is qualitatively different. A bigot can self-define his position about a class of people—but self-differentiation allows the freedom and dignity of the other without feeling threatened or denying the other the right to define self also.

Talking to another person is equivalent to "staying connected." BFST is about emotional process. Merely talking to another person is not equivalent to *functioning* at an emotional systemic level. Staying connected with another person in the system means making an *emotional* connection. That requires a form of communication that is deeper, reciprocal, and affective; not merely giving orders, stating an opinion, stating what we think, or airing our feelings.

Systems theory helps us get out of triangles. Whether we like it or not, we are always in triangles. And if you are in a leadership position, you likely are in some monster triangles that span a couple of generations—they come with the job. BFST is about being able to choose how we will *function* in the triangles we are in.

The leader's job is to lower systemic anxiety. Yeah, good luck with that. An effective leader primarily takes responsibility for managing his or her own anxiety, rather than rescuing the system from the discomfort of anxiety. In fact, a savvy and playful leader understands that pain is an effective motivator for change. He or she knows when to allow the anxiety in the system to climb in order to facilitate emotional process or functioning on the part of those who need to own the anxiety that belongs to them.

Differentiation of Self

I once received an e-mail from a friend who is doing self work. He asked:

I was just wondering if you thought attaining a higher level of differentiation of self lends itself to becoming better able to manage or not get pushed around by one's feelings. I hope this question is not too vague, It's just something I need to get better at so I'm not letting my emotions/reactivity dictate my actions.

My first comment in response was that it is not helpful to think of "levels" of differentiation of self. We want to avoid the misconception that differentiation is a "stage" or "state of being" we achieve or arrive at.

Differentiation of self has to do with our capacity to function in non-reactive ways, rather than in non-thinking ways. For example, it is the capacity to function out of our guiding values, clearly held principles, and our capacity to engage thoughtfully and with intent in our relationships. In other words, it is to be in relationship with others and approach life without being ruled by emotional reactivity.

Here is one description of self-differentiation by Bowen and Kerr:

"The higher the level of self-differentiation of people in a family or social group, the more they can cooperate, look out for one another's welfare, and stay in adequate contact during stressful as well as calm periods. The lower the level of differentiation, the more likely the family, when stressed, will regress to selfish, aggressive, and avoidance behaviors; cohesiveness, altruism, and cooperativeness will break down."[1]

Two ideas that help us appreciate the fact that differentiation of self is more a matter of functioning than "a state of being," are: (1) You can't differentiate self when you're by yourself. Most anyone can be relatively non-anxious and non-reactive by themselves, when they don't have to deal with anyone. But differentiation of self is a product of being in relationship. (2) The real test of one's capacity to practice differentiation of self is how we function in the midst of a challenge. It is in anxious situations, while dealing with difficult people, or, dealing with a challenging situation in a sea of anxiety, that one's capacity to be "self-differentiated" is evidenced.

One reason it's important to make these distinctions is to avoid the mistake of thinking that the goal (or possibility) is that we'll be able to do away fully with our feelings and emotions. The issue is our capacity to function better despite how we happen to feel at the moment or despite our experience of anxiety. So, my friend's thinking is correct: "becoming better able to manage or not get pushed around by ones feelings," and "not letting my emotions/reactivity dictate my actions."

[1]Murray Bowen and Michael Kerr, *Family Evaluation* (New York: Norton and Company), p. 93.

Differentiation and Emotional Maturity

While differentiation of self is a key concept in Bowen Family Systems Theory (BFST) it defines a narrow concept related to functioning. Specifically, the concept is not a description of a state of being or a "stage" a person arrives at or resides in. It describes a way of functioning relative to one's capacity to separate thinking from feeling, thereby being non-reactive and less driven by emotionality when in relationship with others. This facilitates functioning out of one's values and principles rather than anxiety and its derivatives (reactivity, triangling, herding, groupthink, enmeshment, etc.).

Rightly interpreted, Bowen's Scale of Differentiation is a helpful schema for understanding the concept of differentiation of self. The problem lies in how often it is misinterpreted. The scale is a metaphor that depicts a range of functioning. It was not intended to suggest a stage of arrival ("Last year I received my black belt in Karate, and, attained Nirvana." "Within two years I'll be a fully self-differentiated person."), or, even a goal toward which one aspires ("Last month I was 55% differentiated with my teenager. This month, my goal is to achieve 70% on the scale in my relationship with my mother-in-law.").

Emotional Maturity

I find myself favoring the concept of emotional maturity as a helpful frame of reference for many of the elements of differentiation of self. I think there is a direct correlation between a person's emotional maturity and one's capacity for differentiation. Given the fact that emotional maturity is a nuanced and dynamic concept, I also find it helpful to plot it in the wider categories of high, middle, and low levels, rather than on a scale.

Here are characteristics of persons at three stages of emotional maturity:

Persons with Low Emotional Maturity
- They are prone to intense attachments or enmeshments
- They lack self-awareness of emotions or interior life (may not be aware of cutoff, reactivity, stress, or anxiety)
- They lack awareness of, and, have an inability to reflect and interpret family of origin emotional process
- Their Identity is derived from roles, or, constructed or adopted persona (large pseudo-self)
- They tend toward polarization in relationships, with family and others
- They lack capacity to be emotionally neutral. Their emotional stance is irrationally negative (antagonistic) or blindly positive (loyal)
- They often function out of projection (take everything personally)
- They lack capacity for empathy or perspective
- They will tend to act out the anxiety in the family
- Disruptions in their significant relationships typically results in reactivity

- They find it difficult to self-regulate in the midst of and in the wake of a crisis
- They will invest self in a belief system or in people who reassure their beliefs or who promise salvation, status, or privilege
- They lack ability to question or reflect upon the consequences of their behavior
- They lack awareness of how they communicate, or how they do not "connect" with others in their speech or behavior
- They are prone to absorb the anxiety of family or relationship systems resulting in blame, guilt, and psychosomatic symptomology
- They lack an appropriate sense of boundaries (can be prone to over- or underfunctioning)
- They rarely find their self or their voice
- They have a great need for a larger relationship system for managing their anxiety.

Persons with Middle Emotional Maturity
- They may often become too attached and prone to symptoms associated with dependency or fusion
- When not highly anxious they can distance appropriately from the family of origin and establish individual life principles and goals
- In times of high anxiety they will develop symptoms or function out of reactivity; but are able to self-regulate once anxiety diminishes
- They can be aware of interior emotional process if they pay attention
- They have an accurate level of awareness of how they are perceived by others and how their communication is being received by others
- During times of anxiety they will attack, coerce, herd, or use other methods to try and encourage conformity
- They may gossip about people and not deal directly, but they

make efforts to be principled with those who are important to them
- They will unwittingly allow unhealthy and unethical behaviors as they are uncomfortable holding people responsible for what they do
- They will do their (assigned) part to maintain homeostasis in a family or other system (enabler, accomplice, triangle, IP, maintain secrets).

Persons with High Emotionally Maturity
- Highly emotionally mature people are rare. They seem to be the exception rather than the rule
- They tend to rise to positions of leaders, teachers and healers
- They can remain unattached to what and how others are feeling or to reactivity or emotionality
- They have the capacity for seeing others as they are and validating them for who they are
- They have no need to make others into something for their self-gratification, self-validation, or self-worth
- They are clear about their principles and so may stir reactions from others (both positive and negative)
- They function and make decisions based on their principles, ideals, and values rather than on personal need, or, on others' personal needs, predilections, opinions, or demands
- Their emotional field often is experienced as unique, powerful, and different. This can be attractive or experienced as a threat
- They often engender followings that admire or hate them. Either response may be a result of the fact that they don't need others for affirmation or validation
- They tend to be characterized by courage and so are able to challenge rather than pamper, can hold others accountable, and can be prophetic as well as visionary
- They take responsibility for their own goals, their own position, and their own well-being rather than those of others

- In work and relationships their influence is a result of empowering, permission-giving, and collaboration rather than insisting on conformity or setting ultimatums.

Achieving emotional maturity is "lifework." It contributes to our capacity to function characteristically (defined by our character) in a self-differentiated manner in all contexts and in all relationships.

Leadership and the Triangle

A story is told of legendary Packers football coach Vince Lombardi, whose toughness and demand for excellence turned the losing Green Bay football team into a championship organization. The story goes that after a particularly dismal practice he halted the drills and called the players together. He announced that they needed to start from the beginning, by paying attention to the fundamentals. At which point he held up the ball and said, "Gentlemen, this is a football."

One fundamental of Bowen Systems Theory (BFST) is the concept of the relationship triangle. Sometimes we tell struggling novices to the theory, "If you understand triangles you've got 90% of the theory." Consultant and author Margaret Marcuson once interview me on the topic of triangles. It afforded me an opportunity to go back to basics and think about this fundamental concept. Here is a portion of that interview:

Q: *How would you define a triangle?*

A: A triangle is a concept used to describe a relationship structure, or dynamic, between persons. In BFST the concept is used to identify how relationship dynamics manifest anxiety, or, how relationships get patterned. The basic structure of a triangle is simply three persons, or, two persons and an issue. I think what's important to understand about triangles is that it is the dynamic at play within the triangle that is more important than its structure. Too often people focus on the individual parties in the triangle, or, an issue. But it is the systemic dynamic at play within the triangle that is important to understand.

For example, most families are structured the same: parent, parent, and child. Or, spouse, spouse, and issues. That structure obviously sets up the system for a triangle: parent-parent-child. But the natural structure becomes significant when the dynamic of anxiety becomes a factor. It is less helpful, for example, to focus on the personalities of the parties (Bob the dad, Mary the mother, John the child) than it is to focus on the emotional process at work in the triangles that happen in a family system that involves parents and children.

The same is true in a congregational setting. One natural triangle is Pastor-congregation-leadership issues. It is more helpful to focus on the systemic congregational dynamics of that triangle than it is to overfocus on the personality of Beth the pastor, the blue-collar congregation, and the ideas about the pastoral role of leadership either of those parties holds.

Q: *Does "thinking triangles" make leadership easier?*
A: I think I've given up searching for anything that makes leadership "easier." By its nature leadership is complex, difficult, and consists of dealing with problems or creating them.

But yes, understanding the dynamics behind triangles can help a leader function better. By understanding triangles I mean gaining the skill of discerning when you are in one, and, identifying what kind of triangle you are in. It means understanding your own tendencies in functioning when you are in triangles.

Do you tend to create triangles when you are anxious? Is your tendency to act and react, before thinking, when a triangle forms? Do you have patterns of overfunctioning that tend to get you hooked into triangles? Is your tendency to be seduced into triangles? Do you have overfunctioning tendencies that get you stuck in triangles? I think understanding ourselves better and working on our functioning helps us better manage ourselves in triangles.

Q: *What suggestions do you have for pastoral leaders for seeing triangles more clearly? What about how they manage themselves in the inevitable triangles?*
A: Assume that whenever you are speaking with someone in your congregation you are in a triangle. That just comes by virtue of your position in the system. As pastor and leader in the system, that's a given. Nothing is ever about "just" you and the person. Most of our congregational member relate to us primarily on the basis on our position or role in the congregation: "pastor," "rabbi," "priest." Few will ever relate to us on a personal,

individual level. Listen for how often your conversation with a parishioner is about someone else.

Memorize the seven laws of emotional triangles found in Friedman's *Generation to Generation,* and work at being able to recognize the dynamics when you see them.

Learn to discern how you personally experience triangles—some experience them through feelings, others in a more cerebral manner. Feeling-oriented persons may experience triangles as "feeling trapped," or, conversely, as flattering seduction. In contrast, the cerebral types may experience a triangle as becoming confused. If you can learn to become aware of your own manner of reacting to triangles you can identify early when you are in one.

Diagram and visualize. If you find yourself stuck trying to figure out what is going on, take out a pencil and paper and diagram. Diagramming moves you into your cerebral cortex and allows you to gain perspective by separating thinking from feeling. When you diagram you'll be better able to identify the triangles, their nature, and visualize the dynamics at play.

Q: *How does our family of origin influence how we function in triangles?*

A: We acquire our patterns of functioning in relationships, assumptions about people, and our repertoire for handling anxiety in the patterns and relationship triangles from our families of origin. Those patterns remain with us forever.

Our greatest challenges related to triangles have to do with changing the patterned behaviors we learned in our family of origins—outgrowing some, adopting new ones, reinterpreting our experiences of the triangulating dynamics, etc. This is easier said than done. We can all admit how some of the patterns of our family of origin, including triangles, get replicated in our own established families—with spouses, children, even with children-in-laws. What parents, upon hearing what has come out of their mouth after an altercation with a child, has not found themselves crying, "Oh, my Heavens! I've turned into my father/mother!"

Q: *Are there "healthy" and "unhealthy" triangles (or ways of being in key triangles)? If so, what's the difference?*
A: Like all of the concepts in BFST, the concept of triangles is more nuanced and dynamic than we first realize. I think it's helpful to approach triangles as representative of "dynamics" in a system. Therefore, it helps to ask, "What dynamic is behind this triangle?"

A triangle spawned from acute reactivity to anxiety is different from a triangle that is structured as a corrective for the system. For example, a parent who triangles a child into issues related to the parent's marital partner is qualitatively different from a triangle in an organization, say a church, intended to maintain a balance of power. One is a reactive-anxiety triangle and one is a structural triangle. Both types follow the same rules about how triangles work.

I suspect that even the terms "healthy" and "unhealthy" are not accurate to use for triangles. Triangles are a product of the dynamics at play in a system, therefore, they provide a function rather than directly provide content or quality. Triangles are patterns that form as a way to facilitate the dynamic of systemic, or personal, anxiety. In other words: triangles just "are" and they are neither good or bad, nor healthy or unhealthy—they merely serve a function.

I think it's more accurate to approach triangles from the perspective of, "To the extent that triangles in a system facilitate ways for anxiety to work towards a resolution, triangles are helpful to the system. And, to the extent triangles in a system become patterns for binding anxiety or inhibiting change and maturity, then triangles are unhealthy."

Q: *What are some misundertandings about triangles?*
A: Some of the most common misunderstandings about triangles I hear are:

That triangles are "bad." BFST is primarily descriptive, not prescriptive, of emotional process phenomenon. As such, it does not ascribe moral values to concepts. Triangles are not "good" or "bad" they are merely the product of emotional process, typically, anxiety. However, triangles are not always neutral. So it is appropriate to think about to what extent a triangle benefits the health of the system, or, to what extent a triangle hinders healthy functioning in a system.

That the trick about triangles is getting out of them. If you're a leader you likely cannot, nor should try, to get out of the triangles you're in. The issue is being able to respond appropriately, rather than react, in the triangles you are in.

That one can only get "invited" into a triangle. I heard this one recently. I think the error here is that it ascribed intent, motive, and agency to a dynamic. Triangles tend to come about as a result of anxiety and reactivity, which are non-thinking postures. Ascribing anthropomorphic causes are not helpful to understanding what is going on.

That long-patterned triangles are easily changed. I see many pastors get caught by this misunderstanding when they attempt to change a systemic triangle that has its origin in the founding and formation stage of a congregation. While I'm not fond of the metaphor, it's helpful to appreciate that some triangles are "in the church's DNA." Some triangles are a product and element of homeostasis.

That a triangle not of my making is not my responsibility. This is a tough one for anyone in a leadership position. Some triangles come with the job, and while they may not be of your making, when you took the job they became your responsibility to deal with. For example, if you accept the pastorate in a congregation that has a systemic pattern of a triangle between pastor-deacons-concept of leadership which was established during the church's founding, then, as long as you are pastor in that congregation, you will be in that triangle. It comes with the job, it's in the church's DNA, and you can't get out of it.

One big misunderstanding is, **if I know I'm in a triangle I can change another person's behavior.** This one is fascinating in that it highlights the myth of knowledge, which says that once I understand something I'm immune to making a mistake. Most of us know that we can only change the relationship of our side of the triangle (I can change the relationship between me and my father; and I can change the relationship between me and my mother; I cannot change the relationship between my father and mother). But that knowledge doesn't keep us from falling into the trap of trying to change that other side of the triangle. Two insights here: (1) note that the issue is that I can work on changing the *relationship* on my side of the triangle—which does not mean that I can change the person; (2) it is the nature of anxiety in triangles that gets us caught trying to change the other side of the triangle (the relationship between two other persons). And it gets us every time, no matter how much we know about the dynamic!

Q: *What are common triangles in a church and organizational life?*
A: The list can be almost endless:

- Pastor—spouse—and pick-the-issue (one partner's sense of calling, family of origin issues, finances, etc.)
- Pastor—children—church
- Pastor—family of origin—issues related to calling
- Pastor—staff—congregation
- Pastor—deacons—vision for the church
- Pastor—staff person—another staff person
- Pastor—vision—congregational resistance to change
- Pastor—denomination—congregation
- Pastor—family of origin—issue of relationships with church members.
- And, one of my favorites: Pastor—the position of leader—former pastor who refuses to leave the church.

Triangles are endemic. Add your own to the list.

Why Triangles Are "Bad"

One misunderstanding related to the Bowen Family Systems Theory is assigning value statements to its concepts. For example, the notion that overfunctioning is "bad." Overfunctioning, like other behaviors described in the theory is not "bad" or "good," it is merely a function, symptom, or manifestation of emotional process played out in the way people relate to one another. This is why it's more helpful to observe function in the system than it is to assign motives to people's behaviors.

That said we must also accept that all functions manifested as behaviors, while not "good" or "bad", either contribute to the health of the system or work at keeping the system stuck. While we can say that triangles are neither good nor bad, merely one of the many ways systemic anxiety gets played out and structured, we can identify the ways triangles hinder the system's progress toward growth and health. For example, here are ways that triangles are "bad":

- When they promote the development of symptoms in relationships. For example, in a family an underfunctioning parent triangles a spouse and a child to "take care" of the symptomatic adult in the family.
- When they perpetuate chronic symptoms or conflict. For example, when a system—a family or organization—reacts to problems by immediately identifying a scapegoat or identified patient rather than striving toward responsibility and accountability without blaming.
- When they work against the resolution of toxic issues. For example, because of its inability to deal with a willful but esteemed patriarch a congregation perpetually fails to deal with the individual's willfulness by triangling the minister, the patriarch, and the congregation's reticence at holding people accountable.
- When they get so structured so as to block change over time. When triangles get formatted and entrenched, they deprive

people of options, resulting in a lack of resilience. For example, when a triangle becomes part of the structure so that every decision needs to involve one person—whether or not that person has anything to do with the issue or decision. In a small congregation this may involve a "gatekeeper," and, in a family, this may involve a patriarch or matriarch.

While it is not helpful to identify triangles as "bad" it is appropriate to identify when they are detrimental to the health and inhibit the system's capacity to function in mature, responsible ways.

❖

When Is A Cutoff Not A Cutoff?

At a workshop for clergy on Bowen Family Systems Theory and congregational leadership one lingering question came up. When dealing with the concept of cutoffs among clergy, it has become inevitable that someone will bring up the matter of denominations that require their clergy to move every three to four years.

The matter typically comes up related to discussion about the continuing pattern of short tenures among clergy and staff. The backdrop to the discussion is the observation that it takes at least five years for a clergyperson to know the congregation well enough to become its "leader." Most clergy tend to leave their congregations well before then. Many spend the majority of their careers pastoring a string of short-tenured congregations, which means they leave long before they would be able to begin to exert transformational leadership. Often, this results in perpetuating a pattern of cutoffs.

That being the case, clergy from denominations whose polity and/or practice it is to move their clergy every four to five years to a new appointment raise questions about (1) their ability to ever make real differences in their congregations, and (2) the consequences of setting up a system that perpetuates a pattern of cutoffs between clergy and their former congregations.

Emotional cutoff describes the way people manage the emotional intensity associated with a lack of differentiation between the generations or among relationships. According to Murray Bowen, emotional cutoff is *"The process of separation, isolation, withdrawal, running away, or denying the importance of the parental family."*[1] Additionally, Kerr and Bowen wrote, *"The greater the undifferentiation or fusion between the generations, the greater the likelihood the generations will cut off from one another."*[2]

Three factors need to be kept in mind related to the concept of cutoff:

1. There are gradations of emotional cutoff
2. The principal manifestation is denial of the intensity of the unresolved emotional attachment between the parties involved in the cutoff
3. Cutoff is primarily an emotional process — physical or geographic distance is secondary if not inconsequential.

The case of denominationally imposed rotation of clergy as it relates to cutoff and the emotional processes in congregations remains an intriguing matter for study. Right now, I have only questions:

- Is it a cutoff when everyone agrees to the arrangement?
- Is the fact that it feels like a cutoff what makes it a cutoff?

- If the cutoff is imposed by an authoritative body is it a cutoff? Is that a different kind of cutoff and if so, what kind of cutoff is it?
- What are the consequences to a religious body in creating a pattern of short pastoral tenures? How does that redefine or reshape the function of leadership in the congregation? How does it frame the office of the local clergy? What are the benefits and the deficits of the practice? How does the practice frame the relationship that congregations expect to have with their clergy?

[1]Murray Bowen, *Family Therapy in Clinical Practice* (New York: Jason Aronson, 1978), p. 382.

[2]Bowen and Kerr, *Family Evaluation* (W. W. Norton & Co., 1988), p. 271.

Homeostasis Finds a Way

One phenomena of the power of homeostasis is that whenever a leader attempts to bring about change he or she will most certainly encounter sabotage. While we can find some comfort in the notion that reactivity is unimaginative, and therefore predictable, sabotage has a thousand faces. The fun thing about sabotage (if one can be non-reactive about it), is that while we can expect it, we will always be surprised at the forms it takes. For most of us, we never see it coming.

The preacher was annoyed because an elderly man kept falling asleep during his sermon every Sunday morning. So one day he said to the man's grandson, "If you can keep your grandfather awake I'll pay you a quarter every week."

The ruse worked for two weeks. The old man was alert and listened to the sermon. But on the third Sunday the preacher found that the old man had fallen asleep again. After the service the preacher sent for the boy.

"I'm disappointed. Didn't I promise you a quarter a week to keep your grandfather awake?" asked the preacher.

"Yes," replied the grandson, "but Grandpa gives me a dollar a week not to disturb him."

Homeostasis resists change. Every move toward change seems to be met with a countermove in the form of resistance, sabotage, entrenchment, confrontation, opposition, passive aggressive strategies, or sheer stubbornness. Experienced leaders never underestimate the power of homeostasis to reestablish systemic equilibrium.

Will or Willfulness?

What is the difference between having a will and willfulness? The question identifies a point of misunderstanding I hear now and again, namely, that having a will is equivalent to willfulness, or, that because "willfulness is bad" then "will," or exhibiting that one has a will, is bad.

The first misunderstanding is that Bowen Family Systems Theory (BFST) ascribes value labels like "good" and "bad." BFST, like any valid theory, is concerned with describing and interpreting phenomenon, not ascribing or prescribing.

Having a will is akin to intention. It is the capacity of conscious choice and determinate action. Will is what allows us to have agency. Will facilitates self-definition and self-differentiation by a determination to action by choice. When challenges arise, will is what allows us to keep going in the face of sabotage and resistance. To use Edwin H. Friedman's illustration, will is what made it possible for Columbus to press on in his voyage of discovery in the face of tremendous sabotage. When all voices around him demanded that he turn back his ships, he remained focused on his vision and purpose.[1]

Willfulness, on the other hand, is a form of ego-overfunctioning and self-idolatry, which seeks to make others in its own image and impose its values on others. Persons who are willful tend to be invasive and lack respect for boundaries. They are prone to disobedience and exhibit a lack of discipline. They tend to be characterized by fractiousness, unruliness, invasiveness, contrariness, intractability, perverseness, obstinacy, and petulance. Obviously, willfulness is not pretty. Willfulness is the wearisome characteristic of any three-year-old who has discovered the capacity to say "No!" But in adults, especially those in a position of power or influence, willfulness can be very harmful and toxic to relationships and systems.

Willfulness is one interpretation of what constitutes the Unpardonable Sin: refusing to see, or believe, in spite of the evidence, in other words, choosing to remain blind. The frustrating element here, especially for leaders, is that the willful are not amenable to being educated. Because willfulness is a product of the affect (the emotions) trying to reason with it tends to be fruitless.

[1]Edwin H. Friedman, *A Failure of Nerve* (New York: Seabury Books, 2007).

The Facts about Reactivity

Leaders often get caught off guard by reactivity. That's no surprise given that reactivity often feels like a dose of intense raw emotion. That kind of energy goes right to the amygdala, triggering reactivity on the part of the recipient, resulting in a "fight or flight" impulse. A sudden assault of intense reactivity can turn off our rational brain, leaving us with an inability to tap into the resource of cognition—thinking through the problem.

An important skill, therefore, is to learn to recognize reactivity for what it is. The ability to distinguish between reactivity and passion, for example, can help us know how to respond to a person in the grips of emoting. It can be helpful to remember four basic characteristics of reactivity:

- It is not rational
- It is fueled by acute anxiety
- It is a response of the non-differentiated
- It is usually displaced.

Reactivity is not rational. Since reactivity is a non-thinking state of being, leaders can appreciate that trying to "reason" with a reactive person is a waste of time. Setting the emotional tone through self-regulation is a more helpful strategy than trying to compose an eloquent argument.

Reactivity is the product of acute anxiety. Acute anxiety is intense but situational and momentary. Leaders should remember that a reactive response during a time of acute anxiety is episodic and has a short lifespan. Therefore, sometimes, just getting past the moment in a non-reactive posture often facilitates better functioning for all.

Reactivity is the result of a lack of differentiation. Differentiation is not a state of being, it is, rather, a way of functioning in the moment. Reactivity is a sure sign that someone is not functioning in a self-differentiated manner. Therefore, a leader who can avoid feeding off reactivity and functions in a self-differentiated manner in-the-moment becomes a resource to the system, if not to the person in the grips of reactivity.

Reactivity typically is misdirected at the wrong object. Because leaders occupy the position of greatest responsibility in the system they often are the focus of misdirected and misplaced reactivity. Leaders who have the capacity to remember and accept that "This is not about me" can avoid taking it personally or making the expressions, messages, and behaviors of reactivity a personal issue.

❖

II. LEADERS AND LEADERSHIP

Four Goals of the Organizational Leader

Leaders approach their work in many ways. They use various frames of references to inform how they go about their work. Some, for instance, focus on the concept of "leadership style." Others lean toward the leader-as-manager approach while others take the leader-as-visionary track. We can also talk about the "job" of the leader, or, the task, function, role, work, position, mission, charge, etc. But how would you answer the question, "What is the goal of the organizational leader?"

Murray Bowen wrote that one goal of the therapist was to *"reduce the level of anxiety, to improve the level of responsible open communication within the family and to reduce the irresponsible, underground communication of secrets and gossip to others."*[1] He wrote that therapy also involves *"a slow process of differentiation between emotional and intellectual functions and slowly increasing intellectual control over automatic processes."*[2]

If we can engage in playful corollary with leadership in organizations, then four goals of leaders are to:

Work at moderating the level of anxiety. Leaders cannot directly reduce the systemic anxiety of an organization. In fact, attempting to do so directly winds up being manipulative and willful and only manages to increase anxiety (starting with the leader!). But leaders who can function as the non-anxious presence by regulating their own reactivity and managing their own anxiety can help systems self-regulate by modulating the level of reactivity and anxiety the system is experiencing.

Challenge irresponsibility. Reactive organizations often cultivate irresponsibility through groupthink, herding, and an overfocus on "togetherness." Sometimes it appears in the form of underfunctioning, blaming, and victimhood. One goal of the leader then, is to cultivate individual responsibility: challenging people to say what they think as individuals and holding people accountable for their behaviors and performance.

Improve open communication. One of the most effective ways to promote health in an organization is to open up the system's patterns of communication. By-products of reactive, anxious systems are secrecy, mistrust, and gossip. When I became administrator in one highly reactive system I focused on this goal immediately. I intentionally practiced I.R.A. (Information Reduces Anxiety) by flooding the system with communications from my office (It didn't take more than a couple of months for the employees to playfully refer to me as "The Memo King."). I announced that I didn't keep confidences or secrets, and I held people responsible for what they communicated (by way of gossip) or failed to (by way of secrets).

Develop a culture of intentionality. Reactive and stagnant organizations often lean toward inertia. They go about their work in automatic, habitual, unthinking ways. Even if a practice doesn't "work" they'll keep doing the same thing over again merely because, "that's the way we've always done it." Intentionality means that everyone is mindful about why and how things are done. There is no such thing as "a little thing," details matter, and yes, style matters, neatness counts and spelling counts.

Change is a slow process. So one final goal for the organizational leader is a willingness to stick it out and see it through. Essential and developmental changes come about slowly in organizations, and they don't happen without a determined leader willing to be the positive deviant.

[1]Bowen, *Family Therapy in Clinical Practice*, p. 291.
[2]Michael Kerr, "Murray Bowen: Family Therapy in Clinical Practice," in Sidney Crown and Hugh Friedman, *The Book of Psychiatric Books* (New Jersey: Jason Aronson, 1994), p. 395.

Five Personal Resources for Leadership

Purists of Bowen Family Systems Theory (BFST) tend to eschew all notions or frameworks of individualistic perspectives to therapy (like "personality type" or "traits" schemas). They prefer a consistent "systemic" approach that focuses on the system over the particulars of individuals in the system. More weight is to be given to the position and functioning of an individual in a system than to his or her personality because both are more a product of the system than of the individual. By and large I lean toward that perspective, but I think there is something to be said for the capacities that reside in the individual, the person who can be the positive deviant in the system.

After all, one of the most significant contributions of BFST is the concept of differentiation of self. At the end of the day, that's a product of the individual rather than the system.

Especially for leaders, differentiation of self is what enables one's capacity to influence the system—to lead from a principled position rather than as a cog in the system, to act with vision and purpose rather than reactivity, and to foster maturity and responsibility in others. The positive deviant in the system will tend to be the person with the greatest capacity for differentiation of self; the one individual who can think and function above the systemic homeostatic milieu.

As such, I think there are five personal resources every positive deviant leader needs to develop. I call these *personal resources* because in stuck systems they are not the product of the system, but of the individual leader. And let's face it, most systems, most of the time, are stuck in their homeostasis. Here are the personal resources of positive deviants:

Perspective. This is different from "vision," that other important function of the leadership position. Perspective is the capacity of the leader to stand outside the system's emotional milieu. While leaders will always be in the flux of the emotional process of the system they also need to develop the capacity to "step outside" their emotional context in order to gain enough perspective to understand what is (really) going on.

Courage. Leaders need to be willing to stand at the point and be exposed. They need to be visible by being present even in uncomfortable situations. They need to not only be vocal about the vision and goals they have for the system, but must also be willing to be challenged, targeted, misunderstood, and criticized.

Persistence. Leaders who challenge the system toward health (development), growth (change), and integrity (responsibility) will automatically invite resistance, sabotage, and rejection. It hardly matters the "reasons" or motives for those reactive stances; they are merely the functions of anxiety and reactivity related to a challenge to homeostasis. Effective leaders need to cultivate the personal resource of persistence to take on the reactivity and hold the course.

Stamina. Leaders often are surprised at the mindless (unthinking) tenacity of reactivity. Leaders will address an issue and mistakenly assume that it's been resolved. But the fact is that the most willful persons or groups in the system just don't let up. Leaders need to cultivate the resource of stamina to endure those issues that come back time and again. And sometimes, the only way to change a system is to outlast those who remain entrenched.

Ruthlessness. Whether you're a fan of Machiavelli or not, the fact remains that one of the most important personal resources of any leader is ruthlessness. Being ruthless does not mean that one practices the torched earth strategy as a singular approach. Nor does it mean that one's primary stance is adversarial. But on the occasion it is called for, leaders must be ruthless when facing the willful toxic forces whose mindless pursuit is to destroy the system, prey on the weak, sabotage progress, or attack the leader. When there is no reasoning with the unreasonable, leaders must be the ones to restrict, contain, or cast out the toxic elements.

Five Ways to Become a Popular Leader

Every once in a while I need to challenge someone by asking, "Do you want to be liked or do you want to be effective?" In one sense it's a false choice, but, leaders often will have to make a choice along those lines. If the personal need to be liked, affirmed, or appreciated is the primary concern of the leader, effectiveness in how the leader functions in the system will be compromised. For those who would choose being popular over being effective, there are five sure ways to accomplish success:

1. Focus on people's personal needs over the need of the system. Unpopular effective leaders will always seek the welfare of the system, as a whole, over meeting the needs of individuals in the system. But popular leaders will keep their radar out and be sensitive about people's needs, feelings, convenience and predilections, and will focus on meeting those above all else. It's the only way to keep everyone happy, right?

2. Structure your working relationships around triangles. When dealing with persons maintain a triangulated pattern of relationship by always asking and talking about their family or an issue. This will serve to dissipate anxiety by focusing on things other than your direct relationship with persons. People will feel better knowing they will never be called upon to make "I" statements or have to deal with your position on issues. Talking about others is an effective way to manage anxiety.

3. Build cohesiveness in the system by blaming "others out there." If you focus on "them" you can avoid making persons in your system feel like failures because you'll never require that they take responsibility for themselves. If something goes wrong, blame "them." If goals aren't met, blame "them." In fact, you can squash any ambitious idea, save time and energy, and avoid potential failure by declaring that "they" will cause the plan to fail.

4. Take responsibility for people's functioning and for their feelings. There is nothing that will make you a more popular leader than taking responsibility for people's feelings. Take the blame, or, allow excuses for the underfunctioners and incompetents in the system. After all, "the buck" stops with you, right? Effective leaders will only take responsibility for their own functioning and their own position in the system, but they forget that everyone loves a leader who "feels your pain."

5. Finally, popular leaders will work hard at creating a sense of "family" or oneness in the system by getting everyone to think alike, value the same things, share the same opinions and behave the same. Effective leaders always work at fostering personal responsibility and discouraging "group think" or "herding." But that only leads to problems—it's a whole lot easier to lead a herd of cattle than to deal with a system full of mature, self-directed, differentiated individuals who have the capacity to express their own ideas and opinions.

Sometimes leaders need to decide whether they want to be liked or whether they want to be effective. Being a likeable leader isn't too difficult, and everyone likes a "nice guy." Being an effective leader is never easy. But effective leaders are clear about what constitutes true leadership and they have accepted that there's often a price to pay when one answers that calling.

Five Concepts of Leadership

I thought we were happily past millennial-themed emphases (leadership in the new millennium, etc.), but apparently not. I was invited to speak at a conference on "leadership in the 21st century." My dilemma was that I don't think the "new century" is a factor of significance in thinking about leadership, the point being that it misses the point.

The concept of leadership has seen its own evolution in fields of study and in various contexts over the decades. Over the years some concepts have proven more accurate, and helpful, than others. But I think the fundamental reality of what constitutes effective leadership has always been the same. Having said that, we must confess that the caveat lies in how one defines effective leadership. For some, leadership is about getting the job done: *"leadership—the art of getting others to do what you want them to do, when you want it done and to the standards you set."*[1] For others, leadership is about promoting integrity and health so that a system can live into its purpose and mission.

I remain intrigued by the ways people think about leadership. And it's interesting to see how they struggle when presented with a different way of thinking about it. Here are five fundamental concepts about positive deviant leadership that tend to challenge how people think about the leader's role. For many the shift in their paradigmatic thinking is so huge that the first step is struggling to reconcile the disconnect with what they currently believe.

- Personal maturity and integrity are the central factors in leadership, not management technique, organizational philosophy, expertise, or control tactics.
- A leader who is too concerned about consensus and harmony will more likely enable and release the destructive forces and processes in the organization.

- The leader is responsible for his or her position, not for the whole congregation or organization.
- An organization functions best to the extent its leaders are self-differentiated.
- The way a leader helps an organization most is by affecting integrity, promoting personal responsibility, and discouraging dependence.

Taken together and put into practice, these five concepts provide the makings for a positive deviant leader.

[1]John B. Alexander, Richard Groller, and Janet Morris, *The Warrior's Edge: Frontline Strategies for Victory on the Corporate Battlefield* (New York: Avon Books, 1990), p. 49.

Five Just Plain Wrong Notions about Leadership

On occasion I find myself startled at hearing a persistent wrong notion that just won't go away. These notions are sometimes overheard in informal conversation, but sometimes they are offered in lectures or presentations. I don't doubt that the people who express these notions believe them—even if they are just plain wrong. Here are five, often heard, just plain wrong notions related to leadership:

1. Leadership is about having and exerting power and authority. That may be true if one equates leadership with despotism, and it is true to some extent for political power. But the nature of positive deviant leadership is about making it possible for people to commit to the same vision, embrace mutual corporate values, and work together toward shared goals for the benefit of all. As such, leadership is more about one's capacity to influence the system than it is about bossing people or managing resources. And despite appeals to authority or title of office, it remains true that one can only lead the willing.

2. Your personality determines your capacity for leadership. I heard this wrong notion most recently in discussions during a search for a corporate leader. Several persons on the search committee expressed reservations about one candidate because of that person's introverted tendencies. One person argued the importance of having a charismatic personality at the helm. However, leadership is about providing the function the system needs of the person occupying the position of the leader. That function depends on several factors: context, the life cycle of the organization and its stages (transition, developmental, crises, etc.), and the mission and goals of the organization. No one person can provide everything the organization needs of a leader, but the leader needs to always provide what the *position of the leader* requires.

3. Leadership is about changing the organization or system. The idea of leader as "change agent" remains pervasive. While leaders, of necessity, need to deal with change, and in some cases bring about change (developmental, procedural, managerial, cultural, attitudinal, etc.) it is also true that we must balance our ideas about change with the reality of the nature of homeostasis in organizations. I think at best an effective leader can bring about the changes necessary for his or her time in the position of leader in the organization. Those changes need to focus on helping the organization function better (healthier) in carrying out its mission and purpose. A leader whose idea about change is to create an organization in his or her own image is in for a ton of resistance, sabotage, and ultimate failure.

4. Leadership requires knowledge and intelligence. The notion that the primary quality of leadership is expertise totally ignores the reality that leadership is more an emotional-relational function than it is a cognitive-logical one. Certainly we desire our leaders to be intelligent and knowledgeable, and the best ones often are. But the most effective leaders are those who function well within the flux of the emotional process of their organizations and relationships. They do not mistake knowing with doing, or communicating with connecting; and they do not mistake activities with results.

5. People will follow the leader they need. Cesar Millan, the "Dog Whisperer," stated that the human species is the only one whose members follow a dysfunctional leader. The greatest challenge to leadership is the fact that anxious organizations rarely seek out, or have the capacity to listen to, the leaders they need. There is no end to the examples of the fate of prophets whose messages are never received in their time. A prophet is recognized as such after the fact: "Huh. I guess he was right. We should have listened to him!" Systems in crises want to be rescued, and they'll follow anyone who promises deliverance, when what they need is to be challenged to responsibility. Systems in pain want to be healed, and they'll listen to anyone who promises comfort, when what they need is toughness.

Context and Self

Leadership is a function of one's position in a relationship system, and it is mediated by two things: context and self. My observation is that many people ascribe to leadership things that are neither essential nor necessary for effectiveness, like personality, charisma, competence, skills, intelligence, or a particular "style" of leadership. Few seem to appreciate that the nature of the context of the system one is in will influence leadership *more than any other factor.* This is because, first, leadership is always situated—it does not exist apart from its context. And, second, leadership is about the function the system requires of the person in the position of leader.

A family requires functions of its leader that are different from that of the person in the leader position in a congregation or a corporation, for example. Furthermore, the context of a particular system requires different functions of the leader at different times and under different circumstances. In a family, the function of parenting (parents are the "leaders" in a family system) is different when children are young than when they are teenagers. Parental leadership functions are different when the family is stable from when it is in crisis. And a congregation of seventy members in its formation and formatting stage needs a particular function of its pastoral leader different from a congregation of 300 in its prime lifespan stage (for more on leadership functions related to congregational lifespan and size/style see *The Hidden Lives of Congregations*).

The second component that mediates leadership functioning is the self of the leader. By "self" we don't mean things like personality. Rather, we mean his or her sense of identity, capacity for self-definition (stating values, beliefs, and opinions), but more to the point: *the leader's capacity to self-differentiate as the leader of the system* (fulfilling the function and roles of the leader while staying connected to the system). Being a self in the position of leader also requires the capacity to acquire and practice those things uniquely important to that function, like providing vision, practicing courage, and cultivating imagination.

The importance of context and self to leadership is why acquiring a bag of tricks or cultivating expertise in a set of techniques will never translate to effectiveness. Leaders must be adaptive to context and centered on self (though not self-centered). Additionally, there is one other important thing to remember about leadership, and that is: you can only lead the willing. This is why staying connected is critical to effectiveness. The nature and quality of your relationship will determine who moves toward you and with you, and ultimately, will facilitate people's capacity to follow.

❖

Roles vs. Function

I received an e-mail from a Leadership in Ministry Workshops participant asking about the distinction between role and function. This distinction is often difficult for folks to make, but it's simply a matter of defining and delineating terms and concepts. Generally speaking *functions* are specific to one's position in the system, while *roles* are negotiable and interchangeable. Functions have more to do with emotional process, while roles have more to do with management of systemic relationships within the structure of a system.

Here is one example: In a biological family system structure a male is father and provides certain *functions* that only a father can. If that biological father dies or leaves the system he cannot simply be "replaced" by another male. Similarly with the mother in the family: she provides certain *functions* in the family that dad cannot. And if she leaves the system (through death or separation) another woman cannot replace her emotional process function.

One common point of stress in blended families happens when the new parent(s) in the reconstituted family confuse function with role. You cannot replace the emotional function of a biological parent—but you can renegotiate the role(s) the new parent will take in the new family. The "first" dad will always be dad, regardless of how people may want to think about the replacement as "dad." It's why people can have lifelong "issues" with biological parents—even if they've never known them. It's not surprising that issues around a "replacement mom" are more intense, especially if the new mom insists on providing the *function* of "real mom" rather than negotiate a new parent-child *role* relationship in the family.

Another example: In a family, roles can be negotiated. In one particular family the mother may take on the *role* of the "breadwinner" while the dad stays home to be the "homemaker." But their (emotional process) *functions* in the family do not change. Mom is still mom and Dad is still dad. And, on any given year they may switch *roles* (dad gets a job, mom decides to stay home), but their *emotional process function* in the family constellation remains the same.

In a congregational system the dynamic plays itself out in similar but not always parallel ways. I like to say it this way, *"A system understands the functions it needs of its leaders, and the system expects and needs the leader (and not someone else) to provide those functions."*

The most dramatic example is that of the function of vision. Systems, including congregations, expect and need vision to come from the person in the "L position," the leader. If the leader defects in place and does not provide vision the system gets anxious, and sometimes, "lost." And if another person (a staff person, second chair, or a deacon) tries to provide "vision" the system gets confused, and often reactive. Vision is a function of leadership—and the vision for the system resides in the position (not the personality) of the leader.

I've recently had a job change that has put me in the second chair position. During interviews with groups in the organization about my "role" they asked what my vision was. I had to tell them that vision was not my *function*, it belonged elsewhere, with the first chair, the leader of the organization. It was interesting to see the nods of comprehension in the room once that distinction was made. Later, in a conversation with the first chair the topic came up again. The first chair mentioned how important my vision would be to the job. I had to clarify that my function, given my position in the system, was to get clear about the *goals* I would articulate for the institution, but that the vision was something the first chair needed to provide. (for more about the "how" of vision see *The Hidden Lives of Congregations*).

I think the reason it's important to delineate between function and role is that doing so helps us interpret emotional process dynamics better than when we stay fuzzy about those concepts.

A Classic Pastoral Triangle

The most common cases I deal with in my consultations with pastoral leaders involves the classic pastoral triangle. It is "classic" in the sense that it has all of the components of an elegant emotional process triangle: (1) it is generated by anxiety, (2) its source is family of origin dynamics, (3) it is directed at the pastoral leader, (4) its content obfuscates emotional process, and, (5) it invites reactivity.

While the particulars of the classic pastoral triangle vary, the following example follows the general pattern: the pastor receives a communication from a person who is a relative of a member of the pastor's congregation. The communication may be initiated at the door after a worship service, or in the form of a phone call, e-mail, or letter. The person initiating the conversation typically is cut off to some degree from the family member who is the focus of conversation (and who will be made the other point of the triangle). While not always the case, the family member who is the focus of the conversation typically is a close relative, but of unequal status (father to a child; uncle to a nephew or niece; patriarch or matriarch to a misfit (identified patient) or someone who "married into" the family). Part of the dynamic at play is leveraging the influence of the pastor to offset the perceived inequality in status.

In essence, the person approaching the pastor expresses concern for the spiritual well-being of his or her relative. The content ranges from a concern that the person is not "saved" to something vague about "not being right with God." The person triangles the pastor by asking that the pastor visit the relative to witness and get that person saved, to get the person back into the church, or, merely to "pray for" the relative. Regardless, the pastor is "hooked" at this point—after all, caring for the spiritual well-being of the flock is the pastor's job. How can one refuse the sincere request of someone who is genuinely concerned with the spiritual welfare of a relative?

Some pastors will march off immediately (some with Bible in hand) and initiate a visit with the parishioner who is the object of the family member's concern. Others experience a feeling of being "stuck," with a situation that sounds right, but feels a bit "off." These typically sense that they are in a triangle but often cannot identify it. They have taken on someone's anxiety (their "burden") while realizing that it's not one appropriate for them to carry.

Let's examine this triangle to see its dynamic:

1. A family member (Person A) who is cut off from a relationship, or is not able to be in a direct relationship with another family member (Person B) deals with the cut off through religiosity. We do not discount the sincerity of this person's concern for the family member, but we need to appreciate the family of origin issues that may be at play.
2. The unresolved anxiety escalates to the point that Person A triangles in Pastor C. Person A triangles Pastor C using the

content that "hooks" the pastor (religion), but is unaware that the intent of the request is for Pastor C to work on the side of the triangle that constitutes the relationship of Person A to Person B.

3. If Pastor C is not able to self-regulate and takes on the anxiety of Person A, he or she will triangle in issues of ministerial competence (rescuing), will triangle in issues with God, or will get hooked by any number of internal issues (his own relatives who are unsaved or in spiritual peril, issues with family members from whom he or she is cut off and to whom he or she cannot minister, etc.). Or, if Pastor C is prone to overfunctioning, he or she will march headlong into the boundary violation to which the pastor has just been invited.

The one who needs to work at self regulation here is Pastor C, who needs to: (1) recognize the triangle, (2) not get hooked by the content so as to avoid reactivity, and (3) follow the basic rules of triangles, including, work on the relationship on your side of the triangle. So, one pastoral response to anxious Person A might be, "Thank you for sharing your concern. I am Person B's pastor and I certainly care, but tell me, what's going on with *you*?"

Back to Basics: Leadership Rules 101

I enjoy leadership books that revisit the basics. I always find it helpful to be reminded of the fundamentals. Whenever I've managed to get myself in trouble it's because I've forgotten or ignored a basic rule. Here's a non-exhaustive list of Leadership Rules 101 that are worth remembering.

do not photocopy

the right thing. Remember that the most expedient thing is not always the right thing.

 • Your best people are your organization's best asset. Invest in them.

- You are primarily responsible for your stewardship of the organization, not for the needs or happiness of everyone in it.

- Foster responsibility and do not cater to the weakest in the system. If you tolerate poor workers and poor performers you will lose your best people first.

- Leadership is 100% effort done 100% of the time. It comes with the job. The day you decide you're too tired to be the leader, someone else becomes the leader.

- The leader sets the tone for the organization. Leaders who want integrity, transparency, loyalty, and honesty in their organization need to practice them first.

- Leaders are not defined by their business card nor their paycheck, but by their character and their actions.

- Don't get in a business that's not your business.

- When you leave, leave. The future, decisions and welfare of the organization are no longer your responsibility—nor, your business.

- Leave the organization in better shape than you found it.

❖

A Leader's Responsibility

One major trap for clergy leaders is the demand for them to take responsibility for things that rightly are not theirs. This is exacerbated by the propensity of pastors to accept that demand.

After all, they are in the business of "salvation" and redemption, right? As any given member may remind the pastor when challenged to step up to ministry participation, "That's what we hired *you* for, pastor."

In this regard, it's helpful to remember that a congregation is an example of a chronically anxious system. The issue is not that a congregation will experience acute anxiety every once in a while, it's that it *is* an anxious system. Chronically anxious systems take form when the system is structured for it: when someone in the system (typically the leader, or, an identified patient (IP)) is made responsible for someone else's functioning. For example, when pastors are made responsible for people's faith or for the functioning of the staff; when youth ministers are made responsible for the behavior and spirituality of teenagers; when the staff is made responsible for people's attendance and participation in church programs; or, when a committee is made responsible for how much money people give.

The fact of the matter is that the leader can only take responsibility for his or her own functioning, not that of others. To attempt to do otherwise is to set oneself up for burnout, for being willful, for falling into patterns of overfunctioning, or for dramatic and invasive boundary violations. Needless to say the less differentiated and immature persons in the system will not be able to appreciate this stance, especially during times of acute anxiety. The call to "do something about" a staff person or a church member or a committee will often be the demand placed on the pastor of a congregation, followed by the insistence that "it's your job to ensure that people do what they're supposed to." The wise leader knows that his or her job is not to think for or micromanage others, rather, it is to challenge persons toward responsibility and to hold them accountable for their behaviors and choices.

The trap in this rule is that lazy people have great capacity for using good theory for poor ends. For the lazy leader, it's too easy to say, "That's not my responsibility." So it's important to get clear about what _is_ your responsibility and your appropriate function as the leader in the system.

Your Congregation Is Not Your Family

The fact is that, despite the warm metaphor we commonly use, a congregation is not a family. A congregation is a localized, institutionalized expression of a larger social system: the organized religious system.[1] The relationship clergy have with their congregations often leads to seductive enmeshment—even clergy desire their congregations to be family for them, or at the very least "a real community." But until you understand what a congregation is, it's unlikely you'll be able to provide the leadership it needs.

While it's helpful to understand that a congregation is not a family, it often is _more_ helpful to remember that your congregation is not _your_ family. Staying committed to doing one's "family of origin work" will often provide a corrective to this confusion. How often has a pastor not been able to challenge a lay leader who is acting out because that person stirs up emotional process issues related to the father-son or father-daughter relationship in the pastor's family? Or how often has a pastor not been able to provide effective pastoral care for a family in crisis because he finds himself thrust into family emotional processes that strike too close to home? And how many times does a young minister feel crushed and rejected at not being able to be "accepted" by a family size/style church whose members are clearer about family boundaries than the pastor? Unless you are a patriarch pastor of a family-church, it's helpful to remember that your congregation is not your family.

[1]Israel Galindo, *The Hidden Lives of Congregations* (Herndon, VA: The Alban Institute, 2004), p. 21.

Your Congregation May Not Be Your Church

While it is true that we all need community, the paradox about ministry is that, often, the congregations pastors lead may never be their "church." Clergy occupy a particular and unique place in the congregational system, and the things that church members seek and get from their church is often not available to clergy.

I think it is possible to find "church" within your congregation, and I think you can develop intimate personal friendships with congregational members. But issues related to the pastor's position in the system often means that a pastor will never experience his or her own congregation as "church" (sometimes that extends to the pastor's family as well). Issues such as tenure, a disparity in the stages of faith of the pastor and the church, a clash of culture (educational, socio-economic, social, ethnic), or a difference in spirituality styles can often result in differences that preclude most pastors from finding "church" in their own congregations. The challenge for pastors, then, is where to find "church" if not in their own congregations. Finding a peer or support group, therefore, becomes a critical issue. It can make the difference between merely surviving ministry, and thriving.

❖

Ministry Years

During my time in parish ministry I offered spiritual direction for clergy. In the span of two years, four pastors came to me with what I discerned to be the same motivation. Each felt a sense of restlessness, malaise, and vague anxiety about the future of their ministries in their churches. Puzzled by the similarities of their struggles, I sought to determine common factors in their individual lives and widely different church contexts.

The only thing these pastors had in common was that they were either in their seventh or eighth year of ministry in their respective churches. Additionally, none of these pastors had ever had tenure in one church longer than five years. For each, this was the longest they had been in one church as pastor. Could that be the answer? Could it be that what these pastors had in common was the year of ministry at their respective churches? And could that be the source of the restlessness they were experiencing?

After some informal surveys, and many conversations with pastors and denominational staff, I'm convinced that there are important dynamics at work in a pastor's tenure at his or her church. Specifically, I think that there is a particular pattern to the first ten years of ministry for clergy. This pattern is shaped by several factors. First, the nature of corporate relationship dynamics influence how a pastor enters a church, begins his or her ministry, and moves into the position of pastoral leadership.

Second, the pastor's unique relationship with a congregation manifests itself in a predictable ministerial life cycle. The concept of a ministry life cycle suggests that a pastor's experience in the church and parish can be anticipated and managed with some degree of intentionality.

The First Year: "Which door does this key open?"

The first year at a new church, for most clergy, is filled with both excitement and challenge. You work to get to know the people (who's who, who does what, and, if you are a pastor in a small congregation, maybe even who is related to whom). This is accomplished by providing basic pastoral care, visiting with the members, and meeting with as many church groups as possible. You blunder through discovering the "turf" that people think belongs to them, and you manage to put out a few fires—mostly things that were neglected during the interim.

During the honeymoon period, you should work at understanding the history of the church, listening for those stories that define the church's personality and identity. This is a great opportunity to "get dumb" and ask questions you won't be able to get away with later. Taking an observer stance in the first year of ministry at a new church allows you to discover the rhythms, habits, language, and practices of the church that make up its culture.

Ministry management in the first year consists of giving attention to basic pastoral and leadership functions, like fixing administrative problems. These often are simple problems that have festered due to neglect during the preceding pastoral interim period. During the first weeks at my first executive position I was puzzled that every once in a while the secretaries would peek into my office and ask, "Dr. Galindo, a box has just been delivered. Where do you want it?"

My immediate thought was, "It's just a box. Put it anywhere!" But I intuitively realized that what was really going on was that they just wanted an administrative decision to be made. My staff's question had less to do with where to put the box and more to do with the system's relief that there was someone on board whose job it was to make decisions.

During your first year you may tinker with the worship service—but don't tamper with it! Most churches will allow the "new" minister some leeway in tweaking the worship service. After all, they know you went to seminary and assume you know a little about such matters. But most ministers seem too eager to want to make major overhauls to the worship service—mostly, unfortunately, informed more by personal preference than theology. Making too many changes in the worship service threatens a primary source of corporate identity, and the wise pastor will be patient in taking the time to appreciate which worship practices are important to the identity and culture of the congregation before tampering with the local liturgy.

For the beginning clergy, three additional ministry management details are critical. First, negotiate a fair salary package with the church and open a retirement account. Second, get into the habit of reading all those books you didn't get to while in seminary. It's amazing the number of clergy who stop reading after seminary—and it shows in their sermons! Third, ministerial leadership can be an isolating vocation, so, find a support group; it may make the difference between thriving in ministry or early burnout.

The Second Year: "Extending the honeymoon"

In your second year, the honeymoon is about over, so enjoy it and try to extend the good will. With one year's rhythm under your wing, you know what's coming up next as the year rolls on. Now you can anticipate what's around the corner in the life of the church and you can plan ahead and make some proactive changes.

Because you are aware of what's coming next during the calendar year you can anticipate problems and make changes to address them. However, realize that most of those changes will be administrative in nature: fixing things already in place that are broken, improving existing processes for efficiency and effectiveness, shoring up existing structures, and facilitating better communication and integration in church ministries and organization. Basically you'll be addressing people's anxiety points, solving some problems and inconveniences. But if you try to make essential changes, you'll likely run into swift resistance and immediate sabotage.

The truth is that organizations and people don't like to be changed—regardless of what they may say or ask. Some people are starting to get to know you, and most of the members will take your lead with caution. Remember that they've seen pastors and staff come and go. At this stage, they don't expect anything different from you. One pastor shared this experience, "I instituted a major program during my first two years at the church, and I'll never forget what one good deacon said to me: 'I hope this is the right thing for us to do, because remember, I was here long before you got here, and I'll be here long after you're gone.' Meaning, 'Don't leave us with something that's gonna mess us up, or with which we'll have to live with.' Guess what? He was right! I'm gone and he's still there." During your second year of ministry at the church, people aren't ready to make changes that challenge the way they relate, think, or function. Remember, some of them have learned that all they really need to do is wait you out! They've seen staff come and go, so they're not yet willing to invest emotionally in you or your ideas—no matter how logical or rational or appropriate they may be. The wise pastor who is restless for "change" will find ways to make high-profile low-risk changes.

Ministry management during your second year should involve writing a case study of your church. By now you know enough about the church and the people to begin to understand your congregation. Categorize your church in terms of its congregational size, stance, and style. The size of your congregation is an important indicator, not because bigger is better, nor because a larger church is a "more real" church than a small one.[1] Size, while not a factor of fundamental or theological significance to the authenticity or effectiveness of a congregation, is a determinative factor in faith formation. The nature of group formation and relational interactions helps "shape" the faith of persons who are a part of the group. The size of your congregation gives "shape" to its membership. Understanding how that is so will help you know what pastoral leadership you need to provide.

Determine your church's stance. Your church's stance has to do with how it views its mission and ministry. Often a congregation's stance is determined by its immediate context, as with the Urban Ministry Church, the University Church, the Country Club Church, or the Community Church. Sometimes a church's stance is determined by theology, as with the Mission Church, the Pillar Church, the Shepherd Church, or the Outreach Church. Understanding your congregation's stance will get you in touch with its values, myths, self-identity, vision, and practices.

Determine your church's style. Style has to do with the kind of corporate spirituality that your church embraces. Some basic congregational spirituality styles are: Head spirituality, Heart spirituality, Pilgrim spirituality, Mystic spirituality, Servant spirituality, and Crusader spirituality.[2]

Writing a case study for your church will help you begin to articulate your vision for your ministry tenure in your congregation. Notice that the vision you need to work on at this stage is about *your* ministry. The vision you will develop for your congregation will come later. Get clear about yourself first, before you attempt to shape a vision for your congregation.

The Third Year: "Hitting your stride, finding your pace."

During your third year of ministry you're feeling comfortable with your role. You know what needs to be done and you know how to do it. You've gotten to know some of the people in your congregation, and you have some "fans" among them.

By your third year you have a clear enough sense of the church and have gathered enough information to begin thinking about what you need to address in the life of the church. But keep this caution in mind: the clearer you get about the direction in which you want to lead your church, the more creative the resistance and sabotage becomes. The wise pastor knows not to take such resistance personally, understanding that change is just difficult for churches.

If you are a new pastor, and have survived your first pastorate so far, you will have learned more about yourself and about church than you learned in seminary . . . or are likely to learn for most of the rest of your ministry years. This is because the learning curve is steep during these first three years. Since what you need to learn is directly correlated with your survival, the learning is meaningful and powerful. Michael and Deborah Jinkins pointed out the correlation between the amount of new demands placed on beginning pastors in relation to their level of competence. Most pastors will not reach a "comfort zone" between ministry demands and competence till well into their third year.[3] Here's the insight: *it takes three years on-the-job to begin to get competent at ministry.*

Ministry management during the third year at a church involves making decisions about your stewardship of ministry. In order to facilitate the leadership functions that you will need to provide from now on, you'll need to decide what and in whom you will invest your time and talents. The demands on your time and attention are almost endless, and they come from a myriad of places. You can spend your ministry career giving attention to problems, peccadilloes, keeping people happy, managing conflict (or perpetually attempting to avoid them), and any number of things that, in the end, will never yield lasting results or nurture maturity and growth in your congregation. Or you can get clear that you are human, have limited personal resources, and can decide to invest yourself most in those persons, issues, and ministries that will make a difference in the long run.

The Fourth Year: "The year of discontent"

Something happens to most of us during our fourth year at a church: we get restless. It is not uncommon to find ourselves sitting in the office, looking out the window, and wondering what else is out there for us. The fourth year often is a low energy year. The problems in the church that previously were a challenge are now merely nuisances, partly because we discover that we may be solving the same problems over and over. During this year of malaise and ennui, you may find yourself updating your resume and keeping it on your computer, ready to print and mail, "just in case."

One danger faced by many pastors is that at this point they may start paying the price for their lack of study and intentional work in personal growth and professional development. If all you have is a bag of tricks, this is about the time you run out of things to pull out of the bag (and believe me, your congregation will notice). This may, in part, explain the phenomenon of the pervasive clergy turnover in churches before the five-year tenure.

Ministry management during this year of discontent involves recapturing the passion of your calling in the midst of the details and drudgeries of the business of ministry. Now is the time to recommit to reading books and journals, learning new ministry skills, and retooling for the next stages of pastoral leadership. For beginning clergy, now is a good time to think about formal continuing education, like entering a D.Min. program. There's a reason seminaries require three years of ministry experience for acceptance into that program—that's just about the time new clergy are ready to learn different things differently!

The Fifth Year: "The Latency year."

The fifth year of ministry for most pastors seems to be a latency year. People begin to trust you and some even like you. By this time a core group of people actually come to love you. You begin to make your mark in the neighborhood as the local pastor and find your niche in your local professional network. Having taken care of most administrative problems and basking in the renewed good will of a less anxious congregation, you coast a bit. You take initiative in starting some creative programs or ministries and institute some challenging changes. Because you enjoy a certain level of trust from the members, these are accepted with little resistance.

Ministry management during the fifth year includes renegotiating your salary if you haven't already. Most clergy seem so eager to be called to a church that they often have an unrealistic assessment of the financial impact of a move. By now you have a more realistic idea of what your personal financial needs are. Don't do the church a disservice by not helping them understand the realistic financial cost of calling and keeping good staff.

If your church does not have a sabbatical leave policy in place, now is the time to begin the process of educating the church as to its value. Take the initiative in facilitating the process of dialogue that will create a sabbatical leave policy.[4] In conjunction with that process, take an inventory of your personal ministry skills so that you can work on those competencies you'll need for the next stage of your ministry.

The Sixth Year: "Ministry redirection"

Several elements seem to convergence during the sixth year that makes this a year of ministry redirection. If you are a staff member in your sixth year at a church, the senior pastor has probably left by now. The new demands placed on you to provide higher levels of leadership functioning makes ministry challenging, exciting, and scary. Part of your job will include breaking in the interim and, eventually, the new pastor.

During this year it's not uncommon to find both pastor and staff reworking their resumes. Some start taking serious calls from other churches and maybe even make a visit or two in response to searches. This is partly due to the fact that the ministry groove you've worked at creating is now becoming a ministry rut. It's time to begin asking questions of essential changes with your ministry leadership roles and professional goals. Will you stay in the ministry for the rest of your professional career? Do you want to go into teaching? Will you specialize, perhaps in pastoral care and counseling? If you are staff, will you seek a senior pastor position? If you are a sole pastor will you take on the challenges of leading a multiple staff? Is it time to move on to a bigger church?

Ministry management actions during the sixth year can include a good episode of housecleaning. Start throwing out clutter—all that dated stuff that has accumulated on your desk, in your library, in the church organizational structures, and in the church buildings. By now you know whether or not you can throw out that ugly blue flower vase in the sanctuary without incurring the wrath of some church family because it was donated by Great Grandma Alice. Since you know enough about "personal" and "public" turf in your church, you can safely start throwing out things that have accumulated around the church buildings over the years. But perhaps the most important ministry management you'll do in the sixth year is to begin exploring seriously your sabbatical options. Be aware, however, that as you begin to plan for your sabbatical you'll likely encounter some sabotage—from yourself and from your congregation. You'll both experience a certain level of separation anxiety. Remind yourself this is natural and don't let it keep you from benefiting from an important resource for you and your church.

The Seventh Year: "Recharge vs. potential burnout"

If you are pastoral staff, then the new pastor probably is on board by now. The new pastor will either take up the church's vision and support your philosophy and approach to ministry, or, will want to bring in his or her own vision to the ministry. So, it's time to contact the district office, update the resume, and maybe even send some out. If you and the new pastor have meshed and you decide to stay on, you'll need to renegotiate your relationship and leadership function with the church.

If you're the pastor, you'll probably find yourself saying, "I can't believe it's been seven years!" And if you're anything like the four pastors who came to me for spiritual direction, you'll start feeling some stirrings that will blossom full-blown next year.

Ministry management for your seventh year: it's time for your sabbatical. Take it—no matter what.

The Eighth Year: "The pivotal year"

If you have made it to the eighth year of ministry at your congregation and decide to stay, something interesting and powerful happens. You'll feel an emotional shift take place in your relationship with your congregation—and your church will feel it also. In your eighth year of ministry you'll look around and see a whole generation of children who've grown up in the church begin to leave. You'll find yourself begin to officiate the funerals of people who are now friends—not just "church members." And perhaps for the first time, you begin to understand what the metaphor of "pastor" really means.

It is at this point that you realize that the people in your congregation are the products of your ministry, and you begin to wonder about what difference you are making. This is a powerful realization, and it can be overwhelming.

This shift in the pastoral relationship was what drove those four ministers to seek help. Each sensed, intuitively, that there was about to be something different and new in their ministry and within them. They were in touch with the feeling that staying in their respective places of ministry, regardless of the context, would require a new way of relating and ministering. For some, the prospect of being in a more intimate relationship with their congregations was frightening. For others, standing on the border of unknown territory brought up fears concerning their competency.

The Ninth Year: "The year of commitment"

If you navigate well the relational and emotional shifts that take place during the eighth year you can make an emotional commitment to your congregation. You settle comfortably into the realization that this is your church and your home—you belong here. Your congregation, meanwhile, senses whether you are staying or going and will respond accordingly.

During this year you experience a definite shift in your relationship with your congregation. It becomes deeper, more honest, more intimate, and more vulnerable. Because of this, ministry now becomes more about relationships and less about management. And it is that shift that I believe was so frightening for the four pastors who came to me. Ministry as management is easy, really. Clergy training does fairly well in equipping pastors for the management of ministry. But what is at the heart of the Gospel and at the heart of ministry is not management—it is relationship. And being in a more intimate relationship with people is a much scarier posture than standing behind the façade of professionalism and competence in "managing" people. Tragically it seems that too few clergy are able to make that shift. Too many seem willing to abort the possibility of a long tenure at one congregation, opting instead for the safety of ministry-as-congregational-manager in a string of short-term pastorates.

The Tenth Year

If you have lasted this long and have invested well in your ministry tenure, you and your church share a mutual relationship of trust, a shared corporate identity that informs you about who you are, and a mutual vision of ministry. This relationship with the congregation can provide you with the resources to begin working on who you can be. Therefore, because your pastoral leadership function will take on new directions, this is the time to stop recycling sermons. This is the time to begin thinking about the life of your congregation two or three generations into the future.

This is the moment your ministry begins.

[1]See Alice Mann, *The In-Between Church: Navigating Size Transitions in Congregations* (Herndon: The Alban Institute, 1998). See also, Gary L. McIntosh, *One Size Doesn't Fit All: Bringing Out the Best in Any Size Churc.*(New York: Fleming H Revell Co., 1999).

[2]See Galindo, *The Hidden Lives of Congregations* for a full treatment of these congregational frames of references.

[3]Michael and Deborah Jinkins, "Surviving Frustration in the First Years," *Congregations*, Jan/Feb 1994.

[4]See Richard Bullock and Richard J. Bruesehoff, *The Alban Guide to Sabbatical Planning* (Herndon: The Alban Institute, 2000).

Leadership and Family of Origin Emotional Process

I suspect there may be a stronger than usual connection among pastors between their functioning in their family-of-origin and the congregational context. I think most pastors lead their congregations functioning out of their position in, and as a result of the emotional process, of their family of origin than most would care to confess.

For example, one of the most interesting insights you'll likely attain is how much you function in your congregational system out of the birth order in your family. You will likely run a meeting, relate to your staff, and even preach in "the voice" of your birth order more than any other quality or professional practice, technique, management style, or "leadership style." There are deeper issues at work here, like living out the ecclesiastical calling that came from your family or a person in your family (usually "Mom"); or seeking paternal approval, or seeking to meet validation needs, or even, finding redemption. The lesson here: if you want to understand yourself as a leader do your family of origin work!

❖

The Influence of Context

One basic concept of systems theory is that when we enter an emotional system, we become a part of it. Despite notions about rugged individualism and self-determination, the fact is that the systems of which we are a part ultimately influence us more than we influence the systems. In terms of pastoral leadership, the contextual factors of a congregation will have more influence on our function than things we tend to think of as influential. Specifically, things like the congregational culture, the congregational size/style, its spirituality style, lifespan stage, homeostatic forces, and homeostatic emotional process will influence the function and behavior of the pastoral leader more than those things we tend to focus on, like personality, leadership style, expertise, competence, and skills.

For example, as soon as a pastor enters the system in the position of leader, he or she automatically occupies one point of several systemic triangles. Some of those triangles will be systemic "Monster Triangles" that are part of both the homeostasis and the structure of the system. Those monster triangles are multi-generational and likely have been the bane and burden of every pastoral leader to occupy that position in the system—they come with the job! One way to manage one's anxiety is to remind oneself that "this is not about me," even when it feels like it is!

But lest we be too hard on congregational systems, let's remember that we bring our own emotional-anxiety triangles with us into the system, and we'll likely take our personal triangles with us when we leave—much to the relief of our congregation, for it's likely that we've hooked them into occupying a part of our triangles as well.

❖

Firing Staff

I'm always amazed at the level of underfunctioning, if not simple ineptitude, that congregations tolerate from their leaders. I suppose it can be considered the downside of Christian charity. But if you are the leader in the system and you tolerate the low performers and the immature in the system, you'll lose your best people first. There is no quicker way to de-value the good work of the best people you have than to tolerate those who are irresponsible or just not up to par. And in times of crisis and anxiety, your best people will be your most valuable resource when you most need it.

The leader is responsible for the welfare of the system as a whole, including its culture. Fostering a culture that tolerates irresponsibility, incompetence, or willful behavior (insubordination, disrespect, boundary violations, unethical practices) on the part of a few individuals is detrimental to the system. Systems, including congregations, count on their leaders to provide the correctives to toxicity. Effective leaders will make decisions for the welfare of the system over the accommodation of immature or willful individuals.

❖

Maybe the Problem is With You

Have you ever heard a pastor say, "Why is it that no matter what church I got to I always end up with the same bunch of @&#* idiots?!" If you've had a string of dysfunctional churches, the problem is probably with *you* and not the churches. One explanation is that health attracts health and dysfunction attracts dysfunction. We tend to be attracted to certain emotional fields of homeostatic patterns because we like what we know and resist change and challenge. We all have our neuroses of choice; we prefer the pain we know. Emotional and spiritual co-dependency often is the tie that binds clergy and congregations together.

The new pastor was getting acquainted with his new town. He stopped and introduced himself to a fellow gardening not far from the church. After some pleasantries the pastor asked, "So, tell me, what kind of people live around here?"

The old gardener asked, "What kind of people did you have where you came from?"

The pastor replied, "Well, to tell you the truth, I found them to be difficult folk. They were unfriendly, tightfisted, inconsiderate, unappreciative, and sullen."

The old gardener replied, "Yep, well then, I imagine those are the same people you'll find here."

❖

Religion Does Not Trump Biology

There is a point of intersection between one's emotional maturity, capacity for self-differentiation, and one's spiritual maturity. False piety is the last refuge of the willful, and the content of spiritual language often masks a multitude of sins. Knowing how to discern the difference between content of speech and function allows us to respond better to those whose relationship with the church is too wrapped up in issues of pseudo-self or unresolved family-of-origin issues they are trying to work out in the congregational system.

Because religion and beliefs do not trump biology, I think it is not very helpful to spend time questioning people's motives. Regardless of our desire to believe otherwise, most of us are driven more by our emotions than by our rationality. The brain's "Job 1" is survival, physical and then existential. The amygdala is the first organ in the brain to be fully developed at birth, and is the only organ in the brain that is not connected to the cortex. This walnut-sized organ at the base of our brain (just behind the eyeballs) stores emotions associated with memories and experiences (fear, anger, threat (fight/flight), etc.). But because it is not directly connected to the parts of our brain that process cognition it is difficult to connect thinking with feeling when we're anxious. During times of acute anxiety reflecting on what we are experiencing is almost impossible. This is, by design, a good thing. If we come across a hungry tiger we want our amygdala to induce panic, get the adrenalin pumping and startle us into flight, rather than allow our frontal lobe to become enchanted with the aesthetic beauty of the animal and pause in contemplative admiration.

Most people are not aware enough of the cause (the internal emotional process) of their behaviors, feelings, or actions to understand their motivation. I heard one of the most mature, educated and rational church members say to me, after getting caught up the passions of a church crisis, "I don't know what happened to me. I just went crazy." Most of us aren't smart enough to know what motivates us to do the things we do, either. So, it is more helpful to focus on how a person functions than on what he or she says. In other words, focus on emotional process, not content, and allow people their right to go crazy every once in a while.

Choose Facts over Feelings

One of the biggest traps for the immature and undifferentiated leader is the inability to distinguish fact from feeling. Bowen's scale of differentiation posits that the higher you are on the scale the greater your capacity to separate feeling from thinking. Facts have no meaning in and of themselves; they are "just facts." We tend to "interpret" facts by the experience of our emotions; more precisely, by the feelings that we associate with certain "facts" or the perception of fact. If we can separate unhelpful learned emotional responses (like guilt, fear, or panic) from facts, then, the facts become a resource. Facts can give perspective for discernment; anxiety only yields myopia or reactivity.

The next time you are faced with making an important decision as leader, monitor your anxiety and separate fact from feeling. The next time you are confronted with an animated and anxious church member, listen carefully and separate fact (their functioning) from feeling (their anxiety and the content of the message).

❖

Choose Principles over Relationships

This is one of those rules that at first pass sounds "anti-Christian" and counter-intuitive. We are taught that relationship is at the heart of what it means to be Christian and at the center of what it means to be "in community." We are taught that, to be loving, patient, and longsuffering are paramount Christian virtues. But the point here is that a self-differentiated leader holds well-articulated guiding beliefs and values that allow him or her to discern the difference between moving toward a life goal (a life calling or vision) and being enmeshed and held back by those who prefer homeostasis.

The leader often has to make choices based on what is best for the system as a whole rather than what is convenient, or best, for individuals in the system. The critical leadership function of

providing a vision for the system means that clergy often will
need to make a commitment to the principles and values that lead
toward the realization of a vision, or the integrity of the mission,
over the desires or needs of certain individuals in the system. Of
course, the undifferentiated lack the capacity to tolerate distance,
or to appreciate when someone is moving toward their own goals
and dreams. For them, it will feel like abandonment, betrayal, and
callousness and will often result in reactivity like sabotage or
seduction.

Self-differentiation is all about functioning. One
manifestation of the extent to which one is functioning in a self-
differentiated manner is how well one can separate feeling from
thinking. I recently consulted with a normally steady and effective
staff person who found herself stuck on a particular issue. In this
case she knew the right thing to do, and was able to quote the
company guidelines that needed to direct her action, yet, she was
second guessing herself.

By the time she called me to think through the issue she
had triangled in two people in different offices in her organization
(anxiety spawns triangles), reviewed the company guidelines
several times, and called a person in a different company to
double check legal regulations. Despite all that, she still felt stuck.
After working through the issue she gained enough insight to see
how her emotions kept trumping her cognition (actually, in this
instance, it was about how someone else's emotions and anxiety
were feeding her own anxiety and emotions). Despite knowing
what she needed to do, she was stuck not being able to follow
through.

This situation highlights how important it is to hold clearly articulated principles. A clearly articulated principle can be a stay against confusion in the moment when decisiveness and action is called for. In the midst of anxiety, when cogitation and cerebration becomes a challenge, recalling the principles that must guide action can keep one from getting stuck.

Here are examples of principles that can be of help when one needs to decide on one's feet (these are mine; you'll need to come up with your own):

- If you have to choose between convenience and doing the right thing, do the right thing.
- If you have to choose between someone's happiness and doing the ethical thing, do the ethical thing.
- If you have to choose between your values and a relationship, chose your values.
- If you have to choose between what is expedient and what is right, do the right thing.
- If you have to choose between what someone wants and what is best for the system, chose what is best for the system.

What principles guide your actions in times of challenge?

III. CONGREGATIONS AND ORGANIZATIONS

The Middle of the Story

One of the most mystical concepts in BFST is that of the multigenerational transmission process of relationship systems. This multigenerational process is a powerful force at work in biological families and in congregations. When pastors become leaders in their congregations (a type of community and a relationship system) they inherit some things that have come down through the generations they cannot change, and some things they *should* not change—regardless of how un-aesthetic, un-theological, or un-sophisticated they may be.

This multigenerational force is so powerful that often it seems to have the force of a tidal wave or tsunami. Author Edwin H. Friedman has been cited as saying how little change he'd seen in his congregation despite years of effort. *Plus ce change, plus ce meme chose.* "The more things change, the more they stay the same," as the saying goes. If you perform your ministry with integrity you will leave legacies and may make some difference, but in the larger scheme of things, those changes will be minimal; perhaps inconsequential. Enter well and leave well. In the meantime, be a good steward and have fun.

Understand Your Congregation's Culture

Culture is one of the most powerful elements in any system, yet it seems to be one of the least understood and most underappreciated areas that pastoral leaders address. Culture is a corporate dimension that develops over time—it is not "invented." It is multigenerational, and it helps a congregation define "who we are because of what we do."

Culture consists of things like: corporate values, norms, practices, rituals and rites, narratives, artifacts, and ways of being together. Culture, in part, determines how people enter a system and leave it, determines who belongs and who does not, and informs the roles and functions the members of the system play. Unless pastors understand that they carry out ministry within the contextual culture of the congregation I suspect they will never be able to effect developmental change in that system.

Leadership Is Not About Managing Anxiety

You have probably heard this misunderstanding before, but it's so fundamental and such a common misunderstanding that it is worth repeating: "the job of the leader is to lower the anxiety in the system." The function of leadership is *not* about lowering people's anxiety. Nor is it managing systemic anxiety — it is more about managing homeostasis dynamics.

So much systemic anxiety is perceived to be about "change" that we lose sight of the fact that change is the norm, not the exception. Systems will always deal with change — internally and externally driven; evolutionary, developmental, crisis-oriented, planned, etc. The source of anxiety is probably more about the forces of homeostasis than about the reality of change. But the more important perspective is that leadership is about those functions related to one's position in the system, so ultimately, it's about managing one's self on the midst of change and in the face of homeostasis. This is very hard. It is much easier for the leader to perpetually focus on fixing the anxiety in the system, however frustrating and futile the effort, than to focus on his or her own functioning. Indeed, it seems that given the choice leaders will choose the first over the second.

Focus On Principles, Not Issues

Some of the most frequent calls I get from pastors have to do with "issues" in their congregations. This is not surprising since anxious systems (and anxious persons) focus on issues, namely, "content," and the emotional capital they invest in them. Remember that those who lack self-differentiation lack a capacity to distinguish fact from feeling, or, self (identify) from content (belief). It does not take long before the focus on "issues" by ideologues, or those who become willful in the system results in blaming, choosing sides, and finger pointing. If not checked, the anxiety feeds on itself and cycles into scapegoating and focusing on "others." You'll know you've reached a crisis point when the most anxious in the system focus on by-laws, insist on conformity, and make ultimatums.

High-functioning leaders can recognize the difference between content and process, and they can discern what is going on underneath the sound and fury. Low functioning leaders will often go into overdrive and address issues-oriented crises by offering up the scapegoat, re-organizing, micromanaging, parsing a message, or throwing themselves into "action." Look for these reactive responses, and never confuse them with having a plan or taking care of the problem.

Effective leaders will focus on the things that will help the congregation get through a crisis in the healthiest ways. They will focus on: principles, emotional process, functioning, vision, identity, and challenge (as opposed to issues, anxiety, content, crisis, others, and conformity). This requires courage and toughness. This stance of positive deviance will almost certainly ensure that people will not "like" you.

Principles help leaders cultivate the capacity for discernment. Experienced leaders who can operate out of their principles and distinguish between the content of the message and the emotional process at work, learn to discern the difference between willfulness couched in the language of spirituality and the authentic challenge of the prophetic voice. Healthy systems have the capacity to listen to the dissenting voices. This is important because the dissenting voice often is the prophetic voice (it comes from that person able to step outside of the herd and "group-think").

❖

Five Kinds of People

It has been my observation that in times of crisis you can count on seeing five kinds of people emerge. Leaders do well to discern the persons in the system that represent each type, and respond appropriately. Here are the five types:

1. Those who look for miracles. The people in this category want to be rescued and will tend to engage in magical thinking. They form prayer groups, solicit rescuing responses, but will fail in stepping up to responsible action. They may make demands of leaders for a quick fix.

2. Those who criticize but don't offer solutions. People in this group will exhibit reactivity, anger, and find blame. They may seek scapegoats and may rally the most reactive persons in the system into factions. Leaders can be seduced into placating this group or investing a lot of energy and attention to their issues, neither of which will address the crisis.

3. Those who want peace at any price. People in this category have little tolerance for conflict or uncomfortable feelings. They often engage in seduction, seek compromise at the cost of responsible action, and are not able to hold others accountable. They are the ones who cry, "Can't we all just get along?"

4. Those who will abandon the system and run from the crisis. Persons in this group are not an asset to the system. They leave in all manners, quietly disappearing from the scene, or making a fuss to "make a point" before exiting the system. Some are capable of being loud and distracting voices demanding to be heard with no intention of staying around to contribute to positive change. Leaders do well to help the system discern that while everyone has a right to speak, you have to earn the right to be heard. Persons who are not willing to commit to staying to help overcome the crisis haven't earned the right to be heard.

5. Those who step up to responsible leadership. Finally, in the midst of a crisis there will be those who step up to responsible leadership to address the crisis. The people who make up that last group will often surprise you. Many of these are persons on the "fringe" of congregational life. They may be perceived as not being "good church members" because of their lack of participation in every aspect of church life. But often that is because these persons do not stake their salvation on the church. They have a more mature relationship with the church than others who are more dependent on the church and its leaders for their "salvation." And while they do not require their congregation or its leaders to fulfill every need they have for spiritual care, growth, or fulfillment, when their church needs them, they step up, often sacrificially. It is not unusual to see these types of persons recede into the background after the crisis.

Giving Advice

Some time ago someone sent me an e-mail asking for advice on a matter. I wrote back saying, "I don't give advice," though I did provide some resources related to the question. Later, this person asked me to explain what I meant when I said I don't give advice, especially given that he knew I did consulting. "Isn't that what consultants do?" he asked.

On one occasion, at a conference, I dealt with the concept of overfunctioning-underfunctioning reciprocity. At one point I gave a list of examples of overfunctioning. Among them was, "Advice giving." Not surprising from an audience in the helping profession, this point generated a lot of questions and discussion. Since many were "experts" who were sought out for their advice, this news was troubling. Participants wanted to know why giving advice was overfunctioning.

Overfunctioning promotes irresponsibility and dependence. While advice giving may seem to be a helpful act, ultimately it can be ineffective. Here are reasons why:

- Giving advice does not work because it does other people's thinking for them.
- Giving advice can be willful when it imposes one's values or predilection on another.
- Giving advice assumes that the other person does not have the capacity to solve his or her own problem.
- Giving advice denies others the process they need to learn for themselves.
- Giving advice may promote irresponsibility when it is an act of rescuing.
- Giving advice often is an expression of hubris—it assumes we know what is best for another than the person does.
- Giving advice removes the importance of choosing, which is necessary for developing values and for learning.
- Giving advice may be more about managing our own anxiety than about helping another.
- Giving advice perpetuates dependence.

There are more empowering strategies for helping than giving advice. Here are some:

- Empower the other person through challenge.
- Offer resources without endorsement or bias.
- Solicit thinking on the part of the other person.
- Help the person identify options.
- Listen.
- Share an experience.
- Encourage imagination.
- Allow the person to experience the process of thinking through the problem.
- Appreciate that stuckness is one step in the process toward resolution. Do not deny others that step.

The Power of Multigenerational Transmission

The Bowen Systems Theory concept of multi-generational transmission in families, although often difficult to accept at one level, is logically appreciated at another. Families pass along habits, traditions, beliefs, grudges, feuds, genes, and emotional process down the generations. That force can be as powerful as a tidal wave, or as subtle, though influential as an undercurrent. Most of us can readily appreciate how past generations affect contemporary family systems and the individuals in it.

However, I find that many have difficulty appreciating the same for a congregation. This is despite ample evidence of how congregations get stuck, or have conflict, over issues in the past generations (even from many generations past). Generations and members have come and gone since "the incident," yet new members, who have no direct experience of or connection with (and sometimes no awareness of) the issue, will find themselves lict. How is that possible? Edwin H.

; in the present have more to do with what has
vely for many generations than with the logic
ationship.[1]

/here most people fail to appreciate the
tional transmission in congregations: they
ɔgic. But what we're dealing here is emotional
process, not logic.

One pastor I know found himself hurt and disheartened
after experiencing an episode of reactivity in his congregation. He
had been at his congregation for five years and in the past three
years the church saw an increase in new members, including
many young families—the kind of new members every
congregation craves: families made up of young adults with
young children. But predictably, the quick influx of that
population was met with resistance and anxiety as things began to
change: new schedules, new groups, new patterns, new faces, not
to mention all those little children running around putting their
little fingers all over the furniture!

The reactivity took the form of personal attacks on the
pastor and the staff. Many of these attacks came from older
members who were feeling threatened by all the changes. But
some of the attacks came from new members, people who had
joined the church not two years before. Both groups were
attacking the pastor and staff from the same frame of reference:
they were focusing on and accusing the pastor and staff of issues

that had happened fifteen or more years earlier—long before any of these parties had been in the church!

Because congregations are a type of faith community, they operate under many of the same systemic dynamics as families, communities, and similar emotional-relationship systems. New members do not just join an organization; they join a community, with its culture, identity, and *memory*. And part of what any community must do is inculcate new members with these in order to "make them part of the system." It does not take long for new members to become part of the homeostatic milieu of the community. And along with it, they somehow seem to take on the multigenerational transmission of the emotional process of the community, making it, in a real sense, their own.

[1]Edwin H. Friedman, *A Failure of Nerve: Leadership in the Age of the Quick Fix* (New York: Seabury Books, 2007), p. 249.

Anxiety and the Myth of Security

I continue to observe manifestations of how anxiety can lead to a search for security. Even before the current manic anxiety related to the national financial crises, but more so now because of it, I have been observing reactivity taking the form of people seeking certitude in a time of uncertainty. But the fact is that security, guarantees, and certitudes are myths. Helen Keller wrote,

Security is mostly a superstition. It does not exist in nature, nor do the children of men as a whole experience it. Avoiding danger is no

safer in the long run than outright exposure. The fearful are caught as often as the bold. Faith alone defends.[1]

The field in which I work, theological education, has not been immune to the challenges of the times. Seminaries are closing, donations are down, and downsizing, rightsizing, and selling off of assets are common responses across the landscape of theological education and denominations. In the spirit of misery loves company I don't know how many times I've heard someone say something along the lines of, "It is predicted that within the next decade thirty seminaries will close." While the number of seminaries cited and the length of time vary with the speaker, the voice of doom is consistent.

In the midst of this anxiety I observe many seeking the myth of security, mostly manifested in reactivity. People demand assurances, trustees demand accountability, denominations point fingers, and faculty herd by forming clubs or guilds or senates or unions. Some faculty move from one school to another in search of security only to discover that the state of affairs is the same all over—there is no greener grass to be had.

The irony is that in anxious times what is needed is not a search for safety or certitude, but positive deviance in the form of boldness in adventure and imagination. The contrast between these two stances, as applied to leaders, can be striking. The chart below contrasts the insecure leader and the imaginative leader who can be a positive deviant in the system.

The Insecure Leader	The Imaginative Leader
Seeks certainty, guarantees, and safety.	Can tolerate uncertainty and ambiguity.
Seeks answers and solutions.	Ponders new questions and innovations.
Frozen by need for more data, study, and evidence.	Able to take risks and be a trendsetter.
Demands perfection and conformity.	Encourages creativity and novelty.
Looks for the quick fix.	Values persistence and tenacity.
Engages in herding and togetherness.	Encourages personal agency and responsibility.
Exhibits seriousness and secrecy.	Encourages playfulness and openness.
Focuses on and blames "others."	Cultivates personal responsibility in others.
Cultivates rigidity through rules.	Encourages resilience through challenge.
Finds comfort in stagnation.	Finds energy in adventure and curiosity.
Practices denial and gives in to despair.	Practices faith and cultivates hope.
Generates triangles and triangulates.	Engages in direct communication and sets boundaries.

[1]Quoted in, Ruth Fishel, *Time for Joy* (Deerfield Beach, FL: Health Communications, Inc., 1988), p. 146.

Organizational Change

Bringing about organizational change isn't rocket science, but it's not easy either. Those who step into a leadership position that requires institutional and organizational development in effect and by default will need to bring about changes on several levels: administrative, cultural, organizational, relational, and in processes and structures. In other words, institutional development is systemic. Positive deviant leadership requires addressing change in everything all together at the same time.

One skill every effective leader needs for bringing about institutional change is problem solving. Every change brings about a potential new problem, and that problem needs to be solved. For problem solving I know few things more helpful than the Feynman Problem Solving Algorithm. I've found that if I follow it rigorously and to the letter it works every time:

> *The Feynman Problem Solving Algorithm:*
> 1) Write down the problem.
> 2) Think very hard.
> 3) Write down the solution.

Kidding aside, a more helpful list comes from John Champlin who identified seven critical factors for bringing about effective change in an institution:

- The creation and support of clear, attainable goals that are publicized and constantly in use
- The presence of a change agent who can effectively break the equilibrium (homeostasis) holding an organization in place (what we refer to as the positive deviant)
- The use of a systematic, planned process that is open and subject to alteration
- The involvement of the community as an active partner and participant in any major change
- The presence of effective leadership with vision, a sense of mission, a goodly measure of courage, and a sense of the importance of the mission
- A commitment to renewal that disallows compromising for lesser attainments and always aspires to higher levels of sophistication.[1]

[1]See John Champlin (ed), *Paradigms of Political Power* (New Brusnwick: Transaction Publishers, 1971).

Can You Stop Sabotage?

I received a cryptic e-mail from a friend. She was less than a year into a new church staff position. In her e-mail she asked the question, "Can you stop sabotage?" She didn't go into details, but obviously, something was going on (for one thing, it sounded like the honeymoon period was over!). I think it's just as well that she didn't get into specifics. Overfocusing on particulars of personalities, culture, and context runs the risk of moving too quickly into "strategy" (or, as my son likes to put it, "strategery") and overlooking emotional process dynamics.

Sabotage is a common reactive phenomenon we should come to expect. The form it takes, however, is often surprising. Sabotage is an expression of reactivity over a threat to homeostasis. Any time leaders work toward change, of whatever kind, they can expect reactivity. Author Paul Boers wrote this about sabotage:

While sabotage may feel off-putting and distancing, the behavior actually is intended to bring us back into a togetherness mode: the separation of differentiation is too uncomfortable for the system. Leaders must not be surprised, hurt, or offended by this reaction. Leaders are called to responsibility and growth, and this role can be lonely. Leadership includes the willingness to be misunderstood. Our differentiation is not assured until we can respond to sabotage in a healthy way without retribution, rigidity or dogmatism, cut-off, or withdrawal.[1]

So, in answer to my friend's question, no, you can't "stop" sabotage–it's a basic form of reactivity. But, I think there are several ways positive deviant leaders can deal with sabotage:

- Confront it
- Expose it
- Challenge it
- Identify it and name it for what it is
- Sabotage the saboteurs
- Embrace it and use it to your advantage
- Go around it
- Move ahead in spite of it
- Wait it out
- If it's weak and a nuisance you can probably ignore it.

I don't think it's much worth the effort to ascribe motive to saboteurs. As I say, "Never question people's motives." This is especially true when people are acting out of reactivity, which is a non-thinking posture. Additionally, ascribing motive runs the risk that your response will be more about you than the problem or the other person. Ascribing motive to others when we ourselves are reactive is a form of mindreading, and likely a form of projection. It is more helpful to work on observing function and dealing with the emotional process.

For example, when we experience sabotage, and can name it for what it is, we are more capable of thinking, *"Ah, this functioning is reactivity related to a challenge to the homeostasis. Someone is feeling threatened by change. I don't have to take this personally. How can I respond to this person, or to the group, in a way that addresses their anxiety while holding them responsible for how they function?"*

I suspect there are two kinds of saboteurs. First are the unintentional, unthinking persons who are caught up in anxiety and reactivity. They may merely need someone to help regulate their anxiety through staying connected, giving them perspective, or merely giving them an opportunity to share their concerns. The second type, however, is the deliberate, willful saboteur. I think that type needs to be handled differently, and it's worth not confusing the one for the other.

[1]Arthur Paul Boers, *Never Call Them Jerks* (Herndon: The Alban Institute, 1999).

An Effective Leadership Team

As I consult with leaders of organizations, including churches, in these anxious times, I've noticed something new. The new is a shift in focus on the part of leaders from personal to team. This is an interesting shift in that leadership, by its nature, is an isolating enterprise. Leaders need to stand apart, sometimes they stand alone, and often leadership is a lonely state of being.

I've noted, however, an increase in the number of leaders asking questions, and for help, about how they can better tap into their "leadership team" for providing leadership. As one pastor put it, "I don't think I can do this by myself anymore." I think this is a good sign, and a positive further step away from notions of personified (embodied) leadership—those beliefs that see leadership as inherent in an individual, or, in a personality "type" or "style," a notion that misses the insight that leadership is a function and product of the system one is in (see *The Hidden Lives of Congregations*).

Mature and self-assured leaders understand that they cannot provide leadership in isolation. The most effective leaders solicit leadership from those around them. The dilemma for many leaders with staff seems to be how to turn a team (a staff, board, or committee) of followers into a team of leaders. This is a big challenge because (let's be realistic) in most systems there will always be more followers than leaders. Most people in an organization do not want the responsibility that comes with leadership (although that won't keep them from offering their views on how things should be run).

Leadership groups that are effective have the following characteristics, shared among all the members of the group:

- Clarity about and commitment to the mission
- A shared corporate value related to the work and mission (e.g., a "no excuses" mentality, a commitment to excellence)
- The ability to set priority for the welfare of the institution while setting aside personal predilections, preferences, and convenience
- An understanding that it is not enough to say something needs to be done—it *actually needs to be done* and *they* are the ones who do it
- A high level of trust and honesty among the members, allowing for honest conversations, mutual accountability, and challenges toward higher functioning
- An acceptance that leadership means one must lead.

I often hear leaders known for their effectiveness and success say, "I just know how to surround myself with good people." The move from personified leadership to team leadership is a good one. Fortunate is the leader who can surround him or herself with good people. Most of us, I suspect, will not inherit ready-made leaders on a team or staff, we'll need to cultivate them. As with anything associated with leadership it is (1) hard to do, and (2) takes a long time.

How to Deal With a Wall

One of the first dollars I made on a job was knocking through a wall in a New York City brownstone. I used a sledgehammer and it took me an entire day. I was twelve years old and I was paid a dollar in the form of a 1922 silver Peace Dollar. Not a bad deal for a 12-year-old, especially since I've still got that coin and its value has increased over the years.

Leaders who need to address change in organizations often find themselves hitting a wall of resistance. That resistance typically is not overt, antagonistic, and confrontational, rather, it comes in the form of entrenchment, lethargy, passive-aggressive behaviors, and sabotage.

A journalist assigned to the Jerusalem bureau takes an apartment overlooking the Wailing Wall. Every day when she looks out, she sees an old Jewish man praying vigorously. So the journalist goes down to the wall, and introduces herself to the old man. She asks: "You come every day to the wall. How long have you done that and what are you praying for?"

The old man replies, "I have come here to pray every day for 25 years. In the morning I pray for world peace and then for the brotherhood of man. I go home, have a cup of tea, and I come back and pray for the eradication of illness and disease from the earth."

The journalist is amazed. "How does it make you feel to come here every day for 25 years and pray for these things?" she asks.

The old man replies, "Like I'm talking to a wall."

Sometimes leaders may feel that all their challenges and messages of vision and goals are like talking to a wall. The temptation may be to attempt a direct assault to knock down the wall or punch a hole in it. But often, taking the path of least resistance is the way to go. If you want to make progress, sometimes you should stop hitting your head against the wall and just go around it.

How Could They Act That Way?

Times of high anxiety tend to bring out reactivity. There's no question we're living in anxious times, and the increase in consultation phone calls from leaders dealing with staff and employee issues only confirms the obvious. I'm getting an increase in the number of cases of employees or church members "behaving badly." One common lament among hapless leaders is, "I don't understand how they can act that way!"

When faced with reactivity in the form of bad behavior we often get stuck in our confusion about how adults can act badly. The mistake, of course, is in seeking a rationality behind bad behavior. There is no "reasoning" or rationale to reactivity. Therefore, it is of little value to question people's motives for bad behavior. But it is worth asking, "Hmm, I wonder where that came from?"

The Four Goals of Bad Behavior

	Getting Attention	Gaining Power	Getting Revenge	Covering up Inadequacy
Goal of behavior	Getting attention, being acknowledged	Wants to be in control.	Desires to hurt others.	Wants to hide, avoid demands and responsibilities
Typical functioning	Being a nuisance, showing off, clowning, underfunctioning.	Acting stubborn, arguing, tantrums, lying, passive-aggressive behavior, underfunctioning.	Projects own hurt feelings onto others. Defiant, sullen, sore loser, delinquent behavior.	Feels inferior, gives up, and rarely participates, talks a good game but does not follow through, clowning.
Anxiety addressed	Being ignored is to be insignificant.	Feels secure when they can control others.	Getting even with people is the only hope to be achieved.	Fear that others will discover how inadequate they feel/are.
Emotional response sought	Annoyance, acknowledgement. Solicits overfunctioning on the part of others.	Defeated, threatened, provoked. Power struggles.	Hurt feelings, outrage, retaliation, conflict, feuding.	Abandonment, neglect so that they'll be left alone.
Corrective response	Do not reward neediness. Being punitive or demonstrating annoyance is a reward. Only provide attention or acknowledgement when this person does something positive.	Avoid power struggle. Reversals (give them the power they think they want). Join the resistance. Demonstrate respect as appropriate. Ask for their help.	Do not demonstrate hurt feelings or frustration. Provide consequences, but not punishment. Reversals. Provide encouragement when appropriate.	Encouragement, praise for effort. Don't give up on them. Challenge. Do not cater to their weakness.

It can be helpful for a leader to appreciate that while there is no "reason" for bad behavior, there is a *cause* behind people's reactivity expressed in the form of bad behavior. Bad behavior serves a purpose. Some people engage in bad behavior because they intuitively understand the purpose the bad behavior will serve. Others engage in reactivity as a learned behavior that yields a desirable response from others. This is not unlike the three-year-old who has learned that throwing a tantrum will help him get his way.

Generally, there are four goals for bad behavior: getting attention, gaining power, getting revenge, and covering up feelings of inadequacy. Because reactivity is a function of emotionality, reactive bad behavior has as a goal soliciting an emotional response from others. This is why it is important for leaders to be able function from a thinking posture and *respond* to reactivity, rather than *react* to reactivity. That is easier said than done, of course. Leaders benefit from learning to operate at a different level than the anxious flux in the emotional field when in the midst of reactivity. Mentally asking, "What's really going on here?" is a helpful technique for getting below the surface of bad behavior.

The chart on the opposite page identifies the goals of bad behavior, the anxiety they address, identifies the response it seeks, and suggests the corrective response needed.

One fascinating insight is that these behaviors hold true for children and adults. In children the behavior is often easier to recognize, but the same dynamic, and motives, applies for adults. The reason for this is people do not easily change their emotional repertoire over the course of their lives. When we encounter adults acting badly and find ourselves asking, "How can they act that way?" it may be helpful to realize that we're observing an emotionally functional ten-year-old.

We can allow people their right to go insane every once in a while. When overcome by anxiety, any of us will get reactive. Persons whose pattern it is to act out irresponsibly to get attention, gain power, or attain revenge, however, should be called on it. As for persons who consistently act out of feelings of inadequacy, the rule for the leader is to not cater to, encourage, or promote weakness.

The Myth of Competence

Rev. Susan Finster stood at the back of the sanctuary greeting her parishioners at the end of her first "real" sermon at her first "real" church. After seven years as an associate pastor at two congregations she had started the day excited about her first day of ministry as the new senior pastor of Miles Road Church. The service went well and from all accounts the sermon was well received. Susan took to heart the compliments from her new members.

"Great sermon, Pastor," said a member of the search committee.

"Well done," affirmed a deacon.

"Thank you," said a young mother, "that's just what we needed to hear."

But not twenty minutes later, Susan found herself in her office, weeping. She was replaying the sermon in her head, focusing on points in her delivery she thought were poorly done. She wondered if anyone had noticed that her pulpit robe was too large. And she fought back a familiar queasy feeling in her stomach that was always accompanied by a small critical voice that said, "Who do you think you are, anyway?" Fighting the conflicting emotions broiling within her, Susan ended the morning angry at her inability to celebrate the day and her accomplishments. She wondered again about this constant feeling of being incompetent.

Clergy have one of the most challenging careers anyone can hope to take on. Despite theologies of grace and calling to servanthood, congregations expect performance from clergy. This expectation to perform and to provide "results" can become a point of personal and congregational anxiety. Poorly managed, this anxiety can result, ultimately, in clergy burnout, terminations, and congregational frustration. It does not help that American congregations exist in, and often reflect, a culture that values corporate "bottom line" attitudes and expectations of leaders. As a result, clergy themselves often take on those performance expectations.

I have identified among leaders in both the secular and religious contexts what I have come to call "The Myth of Competence."

The Myth of Competence is the attitude, fed by chronic anxiety, that leads to the belief that personal self-worth, relevance, and meaning reside in the external definitions and assurances of being competent in everything one does. It manifests itself in symptoms of systemic anxiety and can result in burn-out and depression.

What the Myth Is Not

In identifying the Myth of Competence, there are certain things that I don't mean. First, I don't mean that incompetence should be tolerated in congregational ministry. In fact, if you are in a senior leadership position, tolerating incompetence merely ensures that it won't be long before you lose your best people. Neither do I mean that we should not be good at what we do. We should, in fact, be setting the example of doing our best for the Lord and the Church. We should strive to do the best we can with the gifts and talents that we possess.

The Myth of Competence does not mean that we should not challenge people to higher standards or fail to hold them accountable to clearly communicated expectations of performance. We should not make excuses for laziness. Truth be told, the lazy have great capacity to use good theory to poor ends. I can't tell you how often I've heard people use the concept of self-differentiation to say, in effect, "that's not my job," or "I don't want to overfunction."

The Roots of the Myth

The Myth of Competence is an occupational hazard that haunts people in leadership, both in the corporate setting and in the ministry context. The myth stems from personal issues related to persons' sense of self-worth, their personal formative history, a deficient personal belief system, and a lack of fully realized self-differentiation or self-actualization. The myth also involves the context and relationships in which leaders finds themselves.

If Susan is to overcome her tendency to operate out of the Myth of Competence, she will need to realize that the myth operates on both the personal and systemic levels. While the Myth of Competence resides at the personal and individual level, it is a systemic issue in that it manifests itself fully in how a person functions and relates to others at corporate relational levels. The myth manifests itself in relationships at work, in the family, in social and community environments.

Susan has long suspected that her nagging feelings of a lack of competence began when she was a child. She's not off the mark. Erik H. Erikson, in his theory of psychosocial development, identified those issues of competence which become central during a formative stage of life. Erikson called the fourth stage of development the Industry vs. Inferiority stage. This stage occurs during our formal elementary schooling years. It is at this developmental stage that we become keenly aware for the first time overtly of family emotional processes, including parental expectations, the performance demands of school, and the messages from peers. Participation in competitive sports and standards of academic performance at school serve to confirm that not all of us are created equal when it comes to skills and abilities. During this stage we may experience an unrelenting pressure to perform.

Because of the nature of congregational relationship systems, persons who function based on the Myth of Competence are very susceptible to systemic pathologies, particularly, those pathologies that take advantage of persons in leadership who fail to function out of a strongly self-differentiated stance. These leaders are ripe candidates for chronic anxiety in various manifestations: hostage taking ("If you don't perform better, we will judge you."), a myopic focus on issues and content ("It's the pastor's preaching that's the problem."), identified patient strategies ("It's the *pastor* who is the problem."), feelings of dependence ("I'd better not rock the boat; no one else will accept me if I fail here.").

Symptoms of the Myth

Functioning out of the Myth of Competence manifests itself in predictable symptoms. For Susan, the two symptoms that consistently got her in trouble as an associate were an over sensitivity to criticism, and, an inappropriate response to flattery. The former gave "power" to the critics in the system and derailed her ability to provide vision. The latter tended to make her emotionally dependent and susceptible to seduction.

Other symptoms include a hypercritical attitude toward others' successes or failures, and a tendency toward blaming. These behaviors put the focus on "others" and foster deflecting repertoires like excuse-making and passive-aggressive behaviors. These responses are counterproductive in that they deflect accountability. Other symptoms are negative feelings about competition, feelings of persecution, inadequacy, insecurity, and "shame."

For some clergy, the Myth of Competence leads to reluctance to take risks often manifested in "poll-taking" leadership and never-ending consensus-building. This leads to a failure in leadership and can, in turn, lead to a lack of personal and institutional growth. Ultimately this failure results in an inability to provide vision. For others, there is the tendency toward reclusiveness and timidity as well as overfunctioning/under-functioning syndromes.

The Paradox of the Myth

Clergy and congregations can fall victim to the societal values that focus on success (typically taken to mean more and bigger), "results," and performance. Miles Road Church, Susan's new congregation, has a reputation for demanding certain performance results of its clergy and staff: high expectations about the quality of worship (especially the preaching), the quality of the day school, the use and appearance of the buildings, and the quality of programs.

Maintaining high standards is a desirable corporate value, but when it is motivated by anxiety it can lead to the trap of the Myth of Competence. In that case, the drive to maintain high standards becomes the drive to be perfect (or to appear so), which carries within it a certain paradox.

Rather than resulting in confidence in the leader, it results in insecurity. You can't always "act" your way into a new reality, which is what Susan found herself doing.

Rather than resulting in effective leadership it results in weak leadership because it feeds into pathological systemic forces driven by anxiety.

Rather than feeling liberating it feels oppressive—having to be "perfect" all the time is exhausting! While those who function out of the Myth of Competence can maintain the façade for a while, the end result is the opposite of what is desired.

Rather than enabling vision it fosters myopia because leaders will stay focused on their performance based on other people's expectations of roles.

The paradox of the Myth of Competence is that **rather than fostering freedom it leads toward controlling behavior** since a leader focused on competence has little tolerance for honest criticism. When the focus of leadership is on the appearance of competence, **rather than resulting in personal and congregational growth, it leads to stagnation.** Once we find the comfort zone of a repertoire or "bag of tricks" we will tend to stick with it and not risk being open to the challenges of growth.

Rather than resulting in maturity, it leads to dependence. Leaders who function out of a desire to appear competent constantly have the radar out for other people's approval. Ultimately, seeking other people's approval can become the motive for making decisions.

Rather than resulting in differentiation, it results in enmeshment as leaders become overly dependent on the system to provide affirmation of self-worth, of values, and of vision. Ultimately, rather than focusing on functioning better, leaders become preoccupied with appearances. Leaders whose drive comes from the Myth of Competence are more concerned with appearing competent than actually being effective. They'd rather receive the affirmation of a system's expectations than engage in challenging the system toward maturity, growth, and integrity.

Moving Toward Wholeness

How do we move beyond functioning out of the Myth of Competence? Certainly it's not easy. On an individual level overcoming the myth may be a lifelong struggle for people like Susan. On a corporate level, systemic anxiety, dysfunctional relational patterns and issues surrounding power make things more complex. Perhaps the most productive starting point for moving toward wholeness begins with the leader. Here are some hints for moving toward wholeness.

First, confess incompetence. Given what we are called to do in ministry, we are all inadequate to the task!

Adopt a functional theology of grace. Living out of the myth of competence may be an expression of a lack of an ability to receive grace, which often also results in an inability to extend grace.

Make personal excellence and relevance the standard of your ministry, not competence. There is a qualitative difference between being driven by a desire to appear competent and a commitment to excellence. Excellence involves setting your own standards based on your personal values and principles rather than working off of other people's expectations. See the accompanying chart for a contrast of these two postures.

Accept failures as progress toward a goal. You know you're doing better if you are willing to accept the risk of failure as a step in the *process* toward goals and vision. Leadership requires vision, vision calls for risk, and failure is often the price paid on the way to ultimately realizing one's vision. Learn to risk the cost of realizing your vision.

CHART: Competence and Excellence Contrasted

COMPETENCE	EXCELLENCE
Locus: External	Locus: Internal
Characterized by anxiety	Characterized by enthusiasm
Feeds on deficits and insecurity	Energized by challenge
Informed by external standards	Informed by internal values
Responsible to others	Responsible to self
Motivated by Expectations	Motivated by impetus and drive
Global and vague	Selective and specific

Seek to understand the origin of the Myth of Competence in your life. One's family of origin is a good place to start as this is where it often begins. Where and from whom did you get the message that you were not good enough? That you'll "never amount to anything"? Children whose parents live vicariously through them are great candidates for the Myth of Competence.

Re-define the role of leadership. Leadership is not being perfect, or infallible, or "strong," or authoritative, or "the best" or "most important." Leadership is about providing the needed functions related to that position: promoting health, maturity and differentiation in others, setting vision, etc. Leadership is more about challenging the system than it is about being perfect.

Given what we are called to do: preach like golden-tongued St. Chrysostom every Sunday, run an organization in a businesslike manner with a volunteer force that is dependent on the good-will of people's generosity, afflict the comfortable, give care to souls that often are unwilling and unmotivated, be the counter-cultural prophetic voice in an often hostile—or worse, apathetic—culture, and be God's presence at all times and in all places, we will always be inadequate to the task. No one is competent enough alone to do what is required for successful ministry. The good news for Rev. Susan Finster, and for us, is that we are not called to do it alone, and that our primary calling is not to results, but to faithfulness.

❖

Changing Others, Changing Self

A very nervous young bride-to-be was counseled by her pastor on a way to stay focused for getting through the ceremony. "Take it one step at a time," said the minister, "When you enter the church tomorrow, you will be walking down the aisle you've walked down many times before. Concentrate on that. And when you get halfway down the aisle," he continued, "concentrate on the altar, where you and your family have worshiped for so many years. Concentrate on that. And as you reach the end of the aisle, your groom will be waiting for you. Concentrate on him."

The advice worked to perfection, and on her wedding day, the beautiful but nervous bride walked smoothly down the aisle in her processional. But people in the audience were a bit taken aback to hear her repeating to herself, all the way down the aisle, "Aisle, altar, him. Aisle, altar, him."

I've noted with interest how often consultation questions I receive from leaders have to do with how to change (alter) others. Even when the request for advice is couched from the perspective of "What do I need to do?" or, "What do I need to say?" the desire is to behave in such a way or communicate in such a way as to get someone else to act differently. This is a natural human response, whether in times of anxiety or at the conclusion of a process of discernment that yields a vision for direction. In times of anxiety we tend to focus on getting others to behave in ways that lower our stress. When we arrive at a vision for a new direction we immediately think about how to get others to change perspective or behavior to support our vision.

The challenge is to accept the power in the truth that essential change needs to begin with the leader. Here are some checkpoint questions worth revisiting whenever we get too focused on finding techniques or strategies aimed at changing others:

- To what extent am I over-focusing on changing others' behaviors rather than monitoring my own internal emotional process?
- Is my focus on other people's behavior a result of having been caught in a triangle?
- Have I checked my personal prejudices, assumptions, or predilections so as not to impose them on others?
- Am I clear that I am only responsible for how I handle my position and not for that of others?
- Am I taking responsibilities for things out of my control (outcomes) or beyond my scope (like the survival and future of the organization)?
- Can I allow others the freedom to take responsibility for how they choose to do their work, make their own mistakes, and work out their own problems?
- Can I discern when I become willful by insisting on consensus, groupthink, compliance, setting ultimatums, and demanding loyalty?

Traits of the Well-Defined Leader

I came across some notes from a presentation by my friend, Ken Hurto, former faculty member in the Leadership in Ministry Workshops (www.leadershipinministry.com). Ken's presentation on leadership was titled "Being a Lighthouse and Not a Bulldozer." In it he used the bulldozer and the lighthouse as metaphors for different styles of leadership.

In his presentation he offered a list of ten traits of the self-defined leader (note his use of "self-defined" as opposed to "self-differentiated"). I think it's a helpful and challenging list that describes something worth aspiring to. Here is Ken's list of traits of the well-defined leader:

1. Knows who she is and what she is becoming. Moves toward maturity.
2. Clear about what he believes and what he values.
3. Works out of a principled perspective.
4. Out front on issues of importance to her.
5. High tolerance for ambiguity and high tolerance for disagreement.
6. Clear personal boundaries.
7. Acts as a catalyst and coach to the system.
8. Achievement-oriented: more concerned with results than feelings
9. Loves life
10. Elastic in relationships; has a broad relationship repertoire.

"Sharecropper" by Israel Galindo. Graphite on paper 9"x11"

Leading From the Right Side of the Brain

I have been a lifelong doodler. In fact, my college class notes look more like sketchbooks than notebooks (and the doodles are the only reason I've kept some of my college notes). Even today pencil and sketchpad are not far from reach in the event an idle moment provides opportunity to doodle. At times doodles have turned into sketches, and sketches into drawings.

The graphite drawing on the previous page, done several years ago, started as a doodle that eventually became a favorite rendering, which today hangs framed in my study. People sometimes say, "Wow, how do you do that?" On occasion my playful reply is, "Well, if you do something every day for most of your life you can get pretty good at it."

Drawing helps artists develop a way of seeing things different than most non-drawing people seem able. Artist and teacher Brian Bomeisler was featured in *American Artist* magazine.[1] Bomeisler (the son of Betty Edwards, author of the best seller *Drawing on the Right Side of the Brain)*[2] teaches the "Global Skills of Drawing" that help students produce more realistic drawings. In effect, he teaches them the principles that help them see the world as it is as opposed to seeing the world as they assume it is.

The global skills of realistic drawing Bomeisler teaches include these five skills:

1. The perception of edges called line or contour drawing.
2. The perception of spaces in drawing called negative spaces.

3. The perception of relationships known as perspective and proportion.
4. The perception of lights and shadows called shading.
5. The perception of the whole, which comes from the previous four perceptual skills.

It occurred to me that all five of Bomeisler's skills of "realistic drawing" are applicable to ministry leadership. Each of those concepts has a corollary when it comes to leadership in ministry. Particularly, they correlate to the way that Bowen Family Systems Theory (BFST) can help us "see" things differently. I like the corollary because, as an educator, one of my tasks in teaching is to move students from naïve understandings to deeper, more "realistic" understandings about the subject under consideration, whether congregations, leadership, ministry, education, or themselves.

1. Leaders need to develop a perception of edges called "boundaries."

A fundamental idea related to the concept of self-differentiation in relationship systems is knowing where one's boundary of self (which includes our personal identity, our values, our thinking, and our feelings) ends and another's begins. People who lack a perception of boundaries tend to have a larger pseudo-self than a core self. In times of acute anxiety and reactivity persons who lack the right perception of boundaries can become willful and invasive. A lack of boundaries can also lead to overfunctioning behaviors (and overfunctioning is always willful).

Effective leaders not only understand boundaries, they are able to set them when needed. For example, healthy pastoral leaders know the boundaries between their families and their ministry. They know the boundaries between personal self (like one's identity) and the pseudo-self that is appropriately shared with the congregational system (like one's role as clergy). Further, effective leaders know how to draw a line in the sand when dealing with willful church members or persons who lack respect for boundaries and act invasively.

2. Leaders need to develop a perception of what you can't see, like "negative spaces."

We can relate this point to the capacity to perceive emotional process. You can't see emotional process directly, but you can see its effect on the system and in the individuals that make up the system. Emotional process is the driving force that makes anxious people do what they do when they engage in automatic responses. It is the force that fuels reactivity and the power behind homeostasis. I define emotional process as, *"The natural, patterned, ways in which an emotional system facilitates the dynamics through which relationships are developed and function in order to maintain homeostasis."*

Being able to see the "negative space" of emotional process is the ability to focus on how people function in a system, rather than focusing on individual personalities or secondary characteristics (like gender, race, ethnicity or cultural heritage). Leading from "the right side of the brain" yields the ability to perceive an episode of reactivity in the context of multigenerational transmission, as opposed to interpreting it as an isolated instance in time. It is the ability to recognize a triangle when you see it (or when you're in it) and being able to discern your place in the triangle and the forces that put you there.

3. Leaders need to develop a perception of relationships.

If ministry (in all its forms) and BFST are about anything, they are all about relationships. One of the most transformative aspects of BFST related to ministry happens when clergy leaders re-frame their perception about their relationship with their congregations and become the positive deviant in the system. Gaining a new perspective on the nature of leadership and of relationships can be freeing, if not redemptive, especially for those caught in the trap of transferring their own family of origin emotional process issues and patterns onto their congregational ministry. We've heard it a thousand times, yet we're prone to forget it: ministry and leadership are about engaging in redemptive relationships. Yet we all too quickly fall into the trap of functioning as if it is about control, results, getting people to do things, or building an organization.

4. Leaders need to develop the perception of shading.

Moving away from black and white, either/or, right and wrong thinking is key to better emotional functioning. The power of leading from "the right side of the brain" (and of systems thinking) lies in the ability to engage in imagination. Being able to work in a broad palate of hues and tones of grays, rather than in black and white, can help the leader entertain options beyond the fight or flight reactivity that is brought on by anxiety in times of crises. The ability to perceive the reality of tones, hues, and shades can help in relationships also. It helps us see people in a new and appreciate that all humans are complex, nuanced, multidimensional, and wonderfully made. It can help us move beyond the temptation to over simplistically ascribe motives to actions and can help us appreciate the influence of emotional process on people's function—a process of which they themselves often are unaware. The way people function, think and feel are colored as much by their family of origin, sibling position, emotional maturity, ability to self-regulate, stage of faith, and level of differentiation as it is by "motives" or cognition.

5. Leaders need to develop a perception of the whole.

This is what "systems thinking" is all about, isn't it? BFST gives us the capacity to "think systems," to see the whole rather than the individual parts. Like an artist who can see the whole canvas and envision how all aspects of composition help bring balance and proportion to the whole, leaders need to see the system's patterns, relationships, dynamics, and forces—rather than merely their effects on its particular objects. Often, it is not what is on the foreground that's most interesting—it is the rest of the components in the "field" that are making us focus on the object of interest that are the most dynamic forces at play.

For example, examine the sketch "Sharecropper." If you look carefully you will note that the composition of the sketch uses the classic "triangle" to force the viewer's gaze toward the eyes of the subject—the viewer cannot help but focus there. But since the "triangle" is part of the composition, which is hidden to the eye, most viewers will not be aware of what the "field" of the sketch is forcing them to look at. Leaders are most effective when they understand "what is really going on" and know how to perceive what others cannot. The capacity of the leader to gaze beyond the horizon line, and see what others cannot, is what we call vision. Changing our way of seeing in order to develop persistence of vision is hard work. But, like doodling, if you do it every day for a long time, you can get pretty good at it.

[1]You can read the article at: http://www.myamericanartist.com/ 2007/02/drawing_without.html
[2]Betty Edwards, *Drawing on the Right Side of the Brain* (Los Angeles, California: J.P. Tarcher, 1989).

Systems Preaching

The position of leadership that a pastor occupies in the congregational system context is unique. Few other organizational systems require the variety of functions called for in the position of clergy, including that of the weekly preaching function. Regardless of whatever else is going on in the life of the congregation or in the minister's own family, Sunday comes around every week, and with it, the need to step into the pulpit and preach.

Here's an insight that can result in positive deviance: preaching is not performance (though it includes that). Preaching, at heart, is a pastoral function that is contextual. It is a pastoral function that is both informed and shaped by the pastoral-congregational relationship of the context. Simply put, the sermon is as much about the preacher, the congregation, and their relationship in the context of being church, as it is about the text. It may be, then, that pastoral leaders would do well to think about approaching their homiletic work from the standpoint of offering "systems sermons."

I cannot find anything overt on what constitutes a good systems sermon in the homiletical literature. But I suspect that a good systems sermon is more about certain qualities than about rigorous attention to a definitive set of rhetorical components that must be crafted into the textual structure of the sermon. Specifically, a good systems sermon is not *about* systems theory. That said, in my thinking, a good systems sermon gives attention to certain aspects of both content and delivery. While there may be more to what makes for a good systems sermon I think it has at least some or all of the following:

- Clarity about the pastor's relationship with the congregation
- Redemptive self-definition
- Awareness and respect of emotional triangles
- Attention to and respect of multigenerational transmission.

Additionally, a good systems sermon demonstrates clarity of the *function* of preaching in the congregational context: Challenge (the prophetic element), Perspective (the particular principles and values that inform one's stance), Theological Content (a confessional stance about beliefs and values), and attention to Identity (the unique corporate culture of the congregation). Most importantly, however, a good systems sermon is, first of all, a good *sermon*.

Clarity of relationship with the congregation

As a seminary professor I get to hear and read my share of "seminarian sermons." It's part of the literary purgatory that comes with the job. What most of those novice sermons tend to have in common are: (1) an over-focus on content and a lack of attention to the mysteries and vagaries of life and relationships, and, (2) a lack of attention to (or awareness of) the relational aspect between the pastor and the flock. These liabilities are inherent and understandable since, respectively, seminarians tend to be young and have not experienced much of life yet, and most have not been in the position of pastor long enough (if at all) to have experienced the unique role of pastor to a congregation. For the majority of seminarians preaching remains, for the most part, performance grounded in text—rather than a pastoral function grounded in a congregational context mediated by the relationship between pastor and flock.

Redemptive Self-Definition

A good systems sermon reflects both self-differentiation and self-definition on the part of the proclaimer. When a pastor of a congregation stands before the flock with messages that communicate, "I will take care of you," "I need you to validate my worth and ministry," "You need me, and would be lost without me," "I bear your burden," or, "I know it all, I'm the expert," he or she reflects not only a lack of self-differentiation, but may reveal a neurotic relationship between pastor and congregation. Self-differentiation allows for the ability to define one's own beliefs and values while allowing the same for the other. Additionally, self-differentiation does not have a need to borrow self unduly from others—individuals, groups, or organizations.

Preacher and professor Barbara Brown Taylor offers good advice on self-definition. *My rule for public truth telling is simple: only say 'I' when you are reasonably sure that those listening to you can say 'me too'. . . . There are several good reasons for following this rule. In the first place, it provides a helpful check on a preacher's natural exhibitionism. In the second place, it recognizes the difference between an audience and a congregation. An audience gathers to be entertained by someone else's peculiar take on truth, and to talk about it afterward. A congregation gathers to be engaged by the common truth that makes them who they are, and to do something about it afterward.*[1]

Preaching Is a Function, Not Performance

Preaching is a function related to the position of the pastor (leader) in the congregational context, and his or her relationship with the congregation, as much as it is about hermeneutical interpretations of the text. Preaching in the congregational setting requires giving attention to systemic issues about the position and function of leader in the system, including: providing vision, ensuring corporate memory (being the communal storyteller), being prophetic (challenging the homeostasis), functioning as the differentiated "head" of the system, guarding the system from opportunistic viruses, etc. I suspect that the overfocus on preaching as performance has a lot to do with the anxiety related to pastors' lack of working on Self, issues of competence, and their uncertain relationship with the congregation.

Attention to and respect of emotional triangles

Leaders occupy the anxiety point of multiple triangles in any system. Clergy who serve in congregations, systems of chronic anxiety, find themselves perpetually a part of the emotional triangles in the congregational system. Some of these triangles are inherited by virtue of office (and therefore, systemic), and some come about due to acute anxiety or personal issues. When caught in an acute triangle, the pastor may be on the receiving end of anxiety or may be the one dishing it out.

The mature and self-differentiated pastor has the capacity to monitor his or her own anxiety and resists bringing anxiety triangles into the pulpit in a willful way. Scholar Walter Breuggemann has warned about the dangers of triangling scripture, God, and the congregation when preaching. Anxious triangles inevitably lead to willfulness. Brueggemann cautions that when that happens in preaching: *In the place of the text, stands the voice of the pastor. That leaves the pastor vulnerable and exposed, for it is only one person's voice. People are not fooled by the substitution when they receive the word of the pastor instead of the voice of the text.*[2] But a pastor may also self-define his or her position in the triangle through the sermon, without being willful (by not making demands, giving ultimatums, or insisting on conformity), thereby shifting the emotional process. Defining self serves to give responsibility back to whom it belongs—and sometimes, anxiety and responsibility belong to the congregation rather than the pastor. The capacity to do this in a responsible and redemptive manner makes for some of the most powerful and transformative moments in a congregation, or at the very least, in the relationship between a congregation and the pastor.

Attention to and respect of multigenerational transmission.

The best "systems sermons" I've heard give attention to the power of multigenerational transmission and the family projection process. These are examples of those "hidden life forces" that are so determinative of relationship systems, yet most people remain unaware of how they influence their behavior. For example, often a pastor's family birth order influences the "systems" relationship component of his or her preaching more than does the delivery style or the textual hermeneutics. It is quite dramatic to hear the voice of a "first born," or that of a "middle child" or a "baby in the family" come through in moments of transparency during a sermon. Because birth order, and family projection process, is so much a part of what constitutes self-identity, pastors often define and position themselves from that orientation in their relationship with their congregations.

Multigenerational transmission and family projection processes have two facets every pastor must give attention to. The first is the pastor's own family of origin related to each. The second is the congregaton's multigenerational transmission and "family" projection issues. On the positive side, the pastor can remind the congregation that, as Church, it does not stand alone, nor does it exist disconnected from its past—its saints and sages, its Abrahams and Saras. But a congregation is also a living community that suffers the ghosts of its Jacobs and Cains. A congregation always exists in the middle of the story, and their pastors enter, minister, and leave from that point. Legacies are celebrated or endured in the present, but shaped for the future, and, "No saint stands alone."

On the negative side, the pastor may have to navigate the family projection process that may be inherent in the congregational system. For example, a tendency to make a martyr or saint of its pastors, or, a tendency to make convenient identified patients of its staff. Another example is an overfocus on the appearance and behavior of the pastor's family. The major dynamic in the projection process is a lack of respect for the boundaries of self between the persons who make up a system. Any pastor who buys into the projection needs or insistence of his or her congregation, and therefore denies authentic self, loses the capacity to be prophetic in the preaching function. Instead, the reciprocal stance may become, "I will be what you need and want me to be."

Preaching, at heart, is a pastoral function that is contextual. And it is a pastoral function that is both informed and shaped by the pastoral-congregational relationship of the context—the congregational relational-emotional system. Simply put, the sermon is as much about the preacher, the congregation, and their relationship in the context of being church, as it is about the text. Until that concept becomes clear, and until systems thinking becomes a part of the way a pastor functions, the sermon event may never provide opportunity to address the emotional process of a congregation.

[1]Barbara Brown Taylor in *The Christian Century* (July 25, 2006): 31.

[2] Walter Brueggemann, "The Preacher, the Text, and the People," *Theology Today* 47 (1990): 237-47.

A version of this article appeared as "What's Systems Got to do With It?" in *Congregations*, Alban Institute (Spring 2007).

Why Are All Systems So Similar?

I was listening to an author speak about his experiences in the inner workings of a major financial firm—one of the several notorious players in the current financial crisis. I was struck at how familiar the company culture, and the speaker's experiences in it was to other corporate contexts. It reminded me of conversations about how universal the Dilbert cartoons are in hitting the mark regardless of where people work—from a large corporate firm to a small business, from a for-profit conglomerate to a non-profit. It begs the question, "Why are all systems so similar?"

We hear hints about this apparent truth here and there. "Business is business, whether you're manufacturing cogs, selling cogs, or selling a service." I've been in certain leadership training seminars where the room held representatives from all manner of contexts, from corporate CEOs to clergy attending to the same latest ideas about how to lead better and manage more effectively.

I have some hunches as to why all systems are so similar:

Relationships systems follow universal rules. I first stumbled across this insight when I picked up a book titled *How to Run Any Organization.*[1] I still have in on my bookshelf, and I must admit it has served me well in all the contexts I've worked in: school administration, corporate, congregation, etc.[1] The second place that idea finds support is in Bowen Systems Theory, which identified universal rules applicable to all relationship systems, from family to business; from government to church.

Complexity emerges from simplicity. While systems and organizations may appear different on the surface they seem all to arise and operate on fundamentally simple rules. The most complex corporation started small and is effective to the extent it can "follow the rules" of its nature. Large congregations look different from small congregations, but ask any pastor and he or she will likely confirm that no matter the size of the congregation, leaders tend to deal with the same problems.

Human nature is the same everywhere. Culture, race, ethnicity, and epochs mediate the universal principles that direct relationship systems, but scratch below the surface and we discover that human nature is the same everywhere, and it has been for a while. Perhaps the best place to see this is in narrative— those stories that are so good about depicting the human spirit and its interior world. Reading the works of the Greek poets and playwrights to Shakespeare, to Chekhov and Dostoevsky to Mark Twain will serve to confirm that we humans laugh, cry, yearn, fear, and hope for the same things—and always have. Idealists who want to create utopias and social organizations that are "totally new" often forget that those new creations will always be populated by the same old people.

The brain is the same everywhere. There may be a biological cause as to why all systems seem so similar. The organic brain, its patterns and its epistemology, are universally the same for everyone everywhere in whatever culture. Hence the educational truism, "Everybody everywhere learns the same way." For example, barring neurological anomalies or or: brain syndromes, every person's brain learns language th way. And, dismissing claims of clairvoyance and ESP, everybody's brain processes phenomenon the same way, for the most part. Given that fact, we can expect that when a group of individuals gather together to form Group A, they're pretty much going to be more similar than different from the group of individuals that gather together to form Group B. That's a great convenience to teachers who find they can effectively re-cycle a well-designed course year after year with little change and still achieve desired learning outcomes with little variance from the norm. For pastoral leaders, understanding the nature of congregations as a relationship system, and the universal principles related to how the relationship dynamics work, can save a whole lot of time trying to figure out one's congregation, and one's place in it.

[1]Theodore Caplow, *How To Run Any Organization* (New York: The Dryden Press, 1976).

Congregations and Pastoral Transitions

Pastoral transitions can be anxiety-ridden times for congregations. Congregations that go through an interim period without pastoral leadership need to navigate transition without an organization's chief resource: its leader. That transition involves many challenges, including, disruption of homeostasis, a shift to inward-focused tasks, and a leadership vacuum.

Disruption of homeostasis

The presence of a pastoral leader often is the linchpin in the primary systemic triangle that facilitates balance for homeostatic forces. The leader can do this by empowering the healthier elements in the system while providing correctives, if not containment, of the toxic and willful elements in the system. Second, the leader's capacity to articulate the vision keeps the system moving forward, and gets people behind that vision, facilitation purposeful movement against homeostasis. Third, often, non-reactive homeostasis is maintained merely by the leader's presence.

But once the pastoral leader is off the scene the influence he or she provided for healthy homeostasis is disrupted. Things become uncertain, the focus on vision wanes, and other forces or dynamics create a sense of disequilibrium. Often, anxiety related to a sense that the homeostasis has been disrupted results in willful reactivity. Persons or groups seek to "get control" of the situation. Some call for immediate action. Others call for "going back" to the way things were before the previous leader. And others will call for a quick fix to identified problems — real or imagined. You may know what it sounds like: "The problem around here is...." Or, "What we need around here is (getting a new church sign, changing the worship service, targeting a new group, getting people to give more money.)" Some focus on an identified patient (IP): "The problem is we have to get rid of staff (the organist, the deacon, the associate, the youth minister, the church secretary, a church member.)"

A change in equilibrium results in anxiety, and congregations (especially those with a low tolerance for uncertainly and ambiguity) want a quick return to a sense of homeostatic stability. It is difficult for congregations to appreciate that during pastoral transitions it will take up to five years for a congregation to "find a new center" that allows for a return to equilibrium.

Inward-focused tasks

During times of pastoral transition congregations, of necessity, need to turn to inward-focused tasks. Pastoral leaders help congregations stay focused on a vision that draws them outward and facilitates creative commitment to the mission. With the exit of the pastoral leader, however, congregations need to shift to internal tasks—one of them being the search for the next pastoral leader. Other tasks include self-assessment of organizational effectiveness, assessing staff needs, reexamining cultural values, achieving clarity of identity, and defining clarity of future goals.

Many of the inward-focused tasks will be more immediate. Congregations will need to decide what to do with their current staff members. They will likely need to reorganize staff assignments and responsibilities. They will need to make decisions about interim pastoral leadership. For example: Will current staff be assigned pastoral responsibilities and authority? Will the church get an interim pastor? What will that person's role be? How much authority will that person have? Will the congregation get an intentional interim?

One danger congregations face during an extended interim period between pastoral leaders is that they may become too intensely inward-focused for too long. That can result in a loss of effectiveness in outward-focused mission enterprises necessary for their effectiveness, if not survival. The issue is not so much shifting to being inward-focused during a pastoral transition (that's just necessary), the issue is not getting stuck there.

Leadership vacuum

Perhaps no other challenge is as great for congregations experiencing pastoral transitions as that of a leadership vacuum. Two statements can help frame this challenge:

1. All congregations are clergy-focused.
2. As much as we would wish otherwise, congregations are highly dependent on paid clergy and pastoral staff for their effectiveness.

That's not to say it is the way things should be, merely a confession that it is the way things are. Given the reality of those two points, congregations experiencing the in-between time of pastoral transitions are in for a challenge.

For congregations that have support staff (associate ministers or program staff) those persons often need to "step up" and take on pastoral leadership functions formerly provided by the designated if not *de facto* pastoral leader (the senior pastor). This can be challenging and scary for staff, but also very exciting and fulfilling. Most congregations will call an interim pastor to provide some of the leadership functions of the office of pastor, but that does not guarantee that the interim will be able to fill the leadership vacuum.

Someone recently asked me what a congregation needs to do during the interim to prepare for the coming of the next pastor. They asked what staff can do in the interim to help the

congregation prepare for the next pastoral leader. My
interpretation is that given the nature of congregations, there's
really not much one can do that will determine the outcome of the
transition, or the outcome of who a congregation calls as the next
leader. But "do something" is a better answer to the question than
"do nothing" in this case:

- Provide congregation-wide education on ecclesiology, the
  nature and mission of the church. It will facilitate
  discernment and provide correctives to less fruitful
  conversations during this time about models, strategies,
  methods, styles, trends, programs, etc. It will provide a
  basis for *theological* conversations with prospective pastoral
  candidates.
- If you get an interim get clarity about responsibilities and
  roles. Re-organizing church structures, cutting programs
  and starting others, and making staff decisions should not
  be included. Those actions tend to (1) result in decisions
  related to the interim's tastes and predilections and, (2) will
  likely hinder rather than help the next pastor.
- Resist trying to fix problems in order to "make it easier" for
  the next pastor. That's just taking responsibility for part of
  the job of the pastoral leader. Let the next pastor fix
  problems the way he or she deems necessary.
- Resist overfunctioning on the part of staff. Hearing
  comments about a staff member like "He's the glue that
  held us together" are flattering, but ultimately not helpful
  for the health of the system.
- Help pastoral staff remember that they are not "the pastor"
  during the interim. I'm not sure why this happens. During
  pastoral transitions associate staff needs to "step up" and
  provide new leadership functions, and that's appropriate.
  But I see too many staff get in trouble when they get
  confused and believe that means they are "the pastor."

Often, it results in a battle of wills with congregants and a loss of effectiveness.

- Avoid the temptation to keep staff from leaving by overpromising, creating a new position or title, bribing, cajoling, wooing, seduction, or enmeshment. Convincing a staff member to stay through the use of seduction may be the worst thing a congregation can do for that staff person. Staff members need to work on taking responsibility for their own calling.

- Remind the congregation that the church belongs to the members, not to the interim, and not to the staff. Church members have a say in what direction the church will go, what values the church will embrace, and how they will respond to God's calling to be the church of Christ. They are responsible for their destiny; no other is, including, the next pastor.

Remember that no matter what you do in the interim, it likely will not determine the outcome of who you get as the next pastor, or whether or not it will be a good fit. The fact remains that times of pastoral transition for congregations are times of acute anxiety. Few organizations or individuals can make good decisions when anxious. Sometimes, we just need to depend on the movement of the Spirit. And sometimes, that's what being Church is all about.

Easier Said Than Done

The concept of the self-differentiated leader is attractive. Those who work toward being self-differentiated leaders strive toward a high goal and often become the positive deviant for the system.

However, while the concept is relatively easy to define, it's easier said than done when it comes to living it out.

First, the concept of self-differentiated leadership consists of several interrelated components, each of which is its own challenge. I use the term components rather than "qualities" to help emphasize that differentiation of self is a product of one's functioning in relationships relative to one's position in the system. It is not, as often assumed, a state of being one achieves. Here is a characteristic list of those components:

- Having and keeping boundaries; knowing where one ends and others begin
- A lifelong process of growing in capacity to become yourself in relationship to others
- Maintaining self-regulation: being non-reactive in the face of reactivity and in the midst of anxiety
- Charting one's own course, setting one's own standards
- Having the capacity to take a stand
- Having the capacity to say "I" (taking personal responsibility) when others insist on "we" (herding, enmeshment)
- Taking responsibility for oneself and for one's position rather than for others'.[1]

It is worth repeating that those are not personal "characteristics" or "qualities," rather, they are ways of functioning in relationship.

Second, as if working on those interrelated components is not hard enough, functioning in a self-differentiated manner always involves doing so in relationship with others. I suspect that one of the most puzzling things to encounter is the paradox that when the leader self-differentiates, two things happen: (1) it solicits the capacity for self-differentiation in some, and, (2) it solicits reactivity in others.

The first response is hopeful and gratifying. While we are warned that the second will happen, we often are caught short by the level of reactivity solicited by the leader's stance toward self-differentiation from those who don't understand it or can't handle it. But if there's any comfort, at least the leader can anticipate the forms the reactivity will take: sabotage, resistance, personal attacks, or seduction. While the forms are predictable one important skill for the leader is learning how to recognize them for what they are. That, too, is easier said than done.

[1]See Friedman, *Generation to Generation*, pp. 27ff.

Pondering the Imponderables

Some of the students in my philosophy course were starting to get annoyed that the professor doesn't answer their questions. More often than not, when a student asked a question, the professor responded, "That's a good question," or, "What do you think?" It did not stopped the students from asking good questions. In fact, as the course went on, the students learned to ask better questions.

Veteran leaders are likely to develop a set of questions they ponder once in a while. Most of those questions are imponderables, questions that seem to have no answer:

- Why is it so hard to bring about change even when people know that it is necessary and even know what changes need to be made?
- Why does it take so long to get things done?

- Why is it that just when you think you finally have a handle on things, someone or something throws you for a loop?
- Why is it that no matter where we go, we seem to run into the same problems and the same problem people?
- Why do organizations tolerate underfunctioners?
- Why do organizations follow dysfunctional leaders?
- Why is it so easy for people to get stuck in groupthink?
- Why do organizations cater to the weaker members rather than reward, affirm, or acknowledge the healthier, stronger members?
- Why is it that a leader's most important challenges are the first to be sabotaged?
- Why is it that the most trivial issues bring out the most passionate and energetic conflict?
- Why can't most organizations get past their original formatting?
- Why is it so difficult for leaders to hold people responsible for their actions?
- Why can't an organization seem to find the leaders it really needs to get it unstuck?
- Why are some leaders drawn to dysfunctional and needy organizations?
- Why do organizations seem to repeat the same dysfunctional patterns, mistakes, poor practices over and over with, seemingly, an inability to learn?
- Why is it that no matter who you put in certain positions or how you rearrange a committee or board, the group will never function any better?
- Why is it that the collective IQs of individuals drops exponentially when they come together as a group?

The Pastoral Leader as Resident Theologian

Students in my online class were studying about leadership in the congregation. From their reading (*The Hidden Lives of Congregations*) they were discussing some of the concepts addressed in the book: (1) leadership is influence, (2) the importance of the leader as resident theologian, and (3) it takes three to five years for the pastoral leader to get to a place of influence that does not derive from his or her position.

By that term "resident theologian" I don't mean that the leader-as-theologian engages in setting forth the one belief expected of all; I don't mean a propositional stance on orthodoxy; I don't mean that the leader's job is to "teach theology." What I mean by the term "resident theologian" is the presence of someone who can model, demonstrate, and train others in the congregation (especially its leaders) to "think theologically."

The perspective is one we've heard before: it's not about providing the answers; it's about teaching people how to ask the better, theological, questions. A resident theologian does not mandate a belief, or insist on orthodoxy—that's what dictators and ideologues do. A resident theologian is one that serves as the resource in the congregation for critical processes of theological discernment, provides correctives in thinking (like pointing out when the congregation is thinking "marketing" rather than "theology" when faced with a decision). The resident theologian cultivates congregational leaders in the practice of critical reflection. He or she equips congregational leaders and members by introducing them to theologians, poets, and prophets and by inculcating in them (and thereby the congregational culture) the language of theological faith.

Framing the function of the resident theologian in that way can help flesh out what we mean, partly, by influence. Influence is mediated by the quality of relationships the leader has (and relationships take time to develop). The nature of one's influence includes shaping the thinking and language of those one leads. This is what the leader does in the meantime between day one and the five years (aside from, as one student suggested, waiting and twiddling one's thumbs—although twiddling thumbs can be an entertaining pastime): they cultivate relationships and they educate the congregation to think like theologians and acquire a theological language (you can't think like a theologian if you don't have the language for it).

Functioning at One's Best

I received an interesting question about Bowen's concept of self-differentiation. The question, an imaginative one, was "What if some day scientists discovered a differentiation gene?" It was fun to ponder, but, genes don't work the way most of us imagine. More to the point, however, differentiation is a product of relationships in a system, the evidence of which is how one functions. If we were to go down the gene therapy route, or more specifically, the biological engineering route related to BFST, then a more likely focus would be how to lower anxiety, and we already have medication for that.

Differentiation is about functioning in relationships. Bowen's Scale of Differentiation posits that one characteristic of the highly self-differentiated person is the capacity to separate thinking from feeling, and, their ability to manage the togetherness-separateness reciprocity in personal and systemic relationships. As I observe leaders who function at their best I identify the following characteristics:

- Balance is manifested in one's life: work and play, family and relationships, responsibility and self-care
- Clear enough about goals so as to not be sabotaged easily
- Clear enough about values so as to not second guess one's own decisions
- Clear enough about principles so as to maintain purpose and agency (self-determinate)
- Can be adaptive enough to change patterns of functioning, especially those that tend to lead toward stagnation or stuckness
- Can stay connected with all parts of the system and does so proactively
- Can maintain boundaries in work (does not overfunction) and relationships (does not own other people's feelings)
- Can receive challenges as opportunities and not problems. In fact, they are energized by a challenge which brings out imagination and creativity
- Can challenge and hold others accountable without assigning blame, denigrating them, or being punitive
- Can avoid personalizing reactivity from others (does not take it personally and does not make it personal)
- Can take responsibility for one's position or job and not for outcomes, or, for the ultimate fate of the organization
- Can seek the cooperation of others without requiring loyalty or personal support
- Can seek the welfare of the system above the happiness or predilections of individuals without feeling guilty.

What other characteristics do you observe in the well-differentiated leader?

50 Skills Every Pastoral Leader Needs To Have

I recently read an article along the lines of "10 Skills Every Man Should Have." I was pleased that I had them all (although it's been a while since I've had the need to weld anything). I wondered what a list of "50 Skills Every Pastoral Leader Needs to Have" would look like. Here's my list:

1. Write a sermon
2. Preach well
3. Lead a meeting
4. Make a hospital visit
5. Make a home visit
6. Read a budget
7. Lead a committee meeting
8. Lead a business meeting
9. Perform a baptism
10. Perform a wedding
11. Lead a confirmation/discipleship class
12. Teach an effective lesson
13. Exegete a passage
14. Keep up with current events
15. Craft a worship service
16. Remember people's names
17. Lead a retreat
18. Write a newsletter column

19. Write a condolence letter
20. Write a stewardship letter
21. Preach a stewardship sermon
22. Lead a staff meeting
23. Deliver a eulogy
24. Conduct a graveside service
25. Tell a scary campfire story
26. Turn off the building fire alarm
27. Talk to teenagers
28. Unclog a toilet
29. Train ushers
30. Entertain the bishop, DS, or deacon chair
31. Set aside time for personal growth
32. Manage personal time
33. Hire (and keep) a good church administrative assistant
34. Fire troubling staff
35. Give away responsibility
36. Delegate
37. Detriangle
38. Tell a joke
39. Handle panhandlers
40. Teach a class
41. Say "No" ten different ways, politely
42. Read a contract
43. Lead a children's sermon
44. Negotiate a bank loan
45. Deal with a contractor
46. Lead hymn singing
47. Select a hymn for a worship service
48. Read a balance sheet
49. Pray.
50. Laugh at yourself often.

How People Stay Stuck

I have been observing several persons in the process of making decisions. Some of the decisions are personal in nature (quitting one job to take another, ending or starting a relationship, going back to school, moving). Others pertain to leaders making organizational or institutional decisions (dealing with employees, closing a program, dealing with a crisis). In only a few of those instances have I observed persons making quick and decisive choices from several options and then moving toward a new direction. Many people struggle through a long winding, angst-filled process of uncertainty and indecision before achieving resolution and finding direction. Several can't identify their options, much less come up with new ones.

A major part of staying stuck has more to do with emotional process. People can't get past the impasse of feelings that block their ability to make choices. But often people get stuck because they cannot think through an issue. We can identify three steps in the process of making a decision: the motivation step, the thinking step, and the decision step. Each of those steps in the process requires the ability to think through the issues at hand. But each step holds the hazard of "faulty thinking" that keeps people stuck. Here is faulty thinking associated with each step:

The Motivation Step

- Trying to reduce the discomfort of dissonance that comes with making a decision
- Seeking to reconcile an internal alignment between the old and the new

- Being driven by feeling obligated to complete a public commitment rather than working out of values, vision and principles
- Being driven by a desire for certainty or security
- Distorting memories or past decisions to make the current decisions seem good
- Soliciting external confirmation that we are about to make a good decision (especially from people who have no stake in the outcome)
- Being driven by the "Scarcity Principle:" the fear of regret at not attaining something that is scarce
- Being immobilized by the "Sunk-Cost Effect:" being reluctant to pull out of an investment of money, energy, or effort even if it has yielded poor results.

The Thinking Step

- Preferring a known probability to an unknown one
- Failing to compensate enough for our own bias
- Elaborating on likelihood: taking uncritical and poorly researched short-cut decisions
- Focusing on short-term benefits rather than long-term solutions
- Seeking more facts for making a decision, even when they are irrelevant
- Failing to critically assess the credibility of a source: seeking input from people whom we are likely to believe rather than those who have expertise.

The Deciding Step

- Being stuck in the "Augmentation Principle:" the belief that evidence for a decision is accumulative
- Using only limited logic in making a decision

- Accepting simple, explainable hypotheses for complex situations and issues
- Failure to use the right strategies for different types of choice
- Deciding by comparing things falsely (apples to oranges).

Making a good decision is about choosing wisely from among options and choices. And while decision-making is both an emotional and an intellectual act, it's important to engage in "right thinking" in order to make right decisions.

"Everything Takes Five Years"

I am often reminded of what my friend Margaret Macuson, author of *Leaders Who Last*, says about bringing about change in congregations, which is, "Everything takes five years."[1] While that's a bit tongue-in-cheek, it's not far from the truth. Over the past four weeks I've had casual conversations with as many church leaders related to how long it takes to get things done in congregations. Each highlighted a different aspect of the dynamic.

Gaining trust takes time. A conversation with a local priest highlighted how long it takes for folks to learn to trust a new leader. Trust is not something that is given totally by virtue of position or office. And if we've followed a leader who has not left well, then gaining trust can be even more difficult. Gaining people's trust takes about five years.

Flushing the system takes time. One recent seminary graduate, only two years out of seminary, is leaving her first church position. She's feeling frustrated that people on her primary ministry committees don't seem to listen to her ideas, don't seem to take her seriously and don't follow her leadership. I shared with her my own perspective that in order to begin to get things done you sometimes have to "flush the system" first. That is, you have to transition out the people on committees that you inherited and start putting in the people you want. Getting the people you want in the right places takes about five years.

Learning the culture takes time. My conversation with a pastor revealed his surprise at how long it took for him to understand some of his church's behaviors and practices. He is in his sixth year of ministry in the congregation and only now is becoming aware of some of the history behind issues, practices, and habits. For one thing, he's noticing that church members are starting to share a different kind of information, one that includes history, stories, and "insider" knowledge that they hadn't shared before. It takes about five years to begin to understand the culture.

Getting settled takes time. I recently met with a church leadership group for a consultation. When I began soliciting basic information about their church I asked how long their pastor had been there. When they said, "Six years," I said, "O.k., so he's been here long enough to have survived a couple of crises and for you to suspect he's going to stay." That got a huge laugh from the group; they recognized the truth in the statement. Later I stressed that at six years, the pastor was in the position "to begin to start" making plans and dreaming about what the church and its ministry can be. Getting settled takes about five years.

Successful congregational ministry requires cultivation and development. Everything takes five years. Sadly, I suspect that too many impatient pastors and ministry staff don't take the long view and end their ministries before they can even begin to start to make a difference. Too often the first crisis (right around the third year) is seen as a personal attack or a personal failure, rather than something that is a matter of course. The key is to get through it and beyond it. The tenacity that can help the leader come out on the other side of the first crisis is what often facilitates the capacity to bring about change.

[1]Margaret J. Marcuson, *Leaders Who Last: Sustaining Yourself and Your Ministry* (New York: Seabury Press, 2009).

The Theory of Hype

Cleaning out some files I came across a listing of businesses for which I had done consultations some years ago. The list was from the early nineties when I was doing more consultations with businesses and corporations than I do now. Going down the list I started checking off those businesses that no longer exist. By the time I finished I'd crossed out over two-thirds of the names on the list. If we were to engage in speculation about the matter we might ascribe two reasons for such a large number:

The first is that it is possible that I was such a poor consultant that those businesses unfortunate enough to take my counsel to heart met with a speedy demise. The second possibility may have to do with The Theory of Hype, which states, *People and institutions whose surface value ("hype") is more than their substance will be driven out by those of whom the reverse is true.*

Reflecting back on those defunct organizations, and their leaders, I think the second applies. All of those companies, and their leaders, subscribed to the notion "An ounce of presentation is worth a ton of production." As I recalled, every one of the organizations who called me in for a consultation was more interested in how to hype, spin, brand, and sell their company's image than about being more productive or working towards the integrity between their mission and their work ethic or work practices. They were more concerned about working at appearing good than doing good work.

Focusing on hype rather than mission or effectiveness will not carry any organization over the long haul. It won't take long for it to be replaced by another who can actually deliver on what it promises. I think the same applies to congregations and their leaders.

So, what is your congregation, and its leaders, most concerned about? Its hype or its mission and effectiveness?

Novelty, Reflection, and Learning

I've observed that most people settle into a professional routine (a rut, really) that intersects with the arrival at a certain level of competence. Once they learn the job and find efficient (if not effective) ways of doing it, they'll rarely stray from the patterned practices of routine. It is a case of "If it's not broke, don't fix it." But it is also a case of a non-thinking stance, "We've always done it this way before." The danger is that a failure to reflect on one's practices leads to stagnation and stifles the imagination. Donald Schon, in *The Reflective Practitioner* wrote:

Much reflection-in-action hinges on the experience of surprise. When intuitive, spontaneous performance yields nothing more than the results expected for it, then we tend not to think about it. But when intuitive performance leads to surprises, pleasing and promising or unwanted, we may respond by reflection-in-action.[1]

Being caught up in non-thinking routine and habits may be a product of homeostasis; it may be a question of being caught in the lethargy of resistance to change. Imagination and creativity take energy. They require lifting one's sight beyond the mundane day-to-day grind to glimpse the horizon. Only then may we gain perspective and perceive ways of doing things differently. So, every once is a while it is worth injecting some novelty into a workday or standing on tiptoes to peek over the horizon.

[1]Donald A. Schon, *The Reflective Practitioner: How Professionals Think in Action* (New York: Basic Books, 1984), p. 56.

How to Handle a Dysfunctional Staff Colleague

Few things seem as frustrating to pastoral leaders as working with underfunctioning or incompetent staff persons. Ironically, the overwhelming feeling by supervisors is one of powerlessness in the face of ineptitude. Other common dilemmas that get supervisors stuck are: the trap of needing to be liked, wanting to be seen as "fair" and "understanding," and the fear of making a tough decision that will affect another's life.

Let's face it, there's no easy way to handle a difficult staff situation. If you are the leader, handling tough problems and making hard decisions just comes with the job. When it comes to handling dysfunctional staff I have little advice to offer for dealing with internal emotional angst, insecurity, or self-doubt. But here are some pointers of a more pragmatic nature I've found helpful when dealing with troubling staff:

- Pray for them. It will help you get past your own anger.
- Pray for patience for yourself. Impatience, and the reactivity that follows its wake, is a sure sign you've taken the situation personally.
- Practice grace in trying to understand and accept the person despite their performance. I've found practicing Carl Roger's "unconditional positive regard" a great way to separate poor performance from personal worth.[1] It is possible to preserve a staff person's dignity while holding him or her accountable.
- Express appreciation when they do something right (publicly and privately). Some people seem to think that giving a compliment is equivalent to losing "chips." People need to know when they've done a good job, as much as when they've done less than the best.
- Share your concerns honestly with the staff person. I'm always surprised that nine times out of ten, the answer to the question, "Have you talked with the staff person about your frustration?" is, "No."
- Encourage them to grow professionally and personally. Those who take you up on this invitation in tangible ways earn a second chance. Those who do not are giving evidence that there's likely little motivation on their part to contribute to the health of the organization through their own growth.
- Be clear about your expectations for a personal and professional working relationship
- Don't take responsibility for their mistakes; give them freedom to fail (and learn). In other words, resist

overfunctioning, and, don't take it personally. Poor performance on their part is not necessarily a poor reflection on you.

- Be frank with staff and supervising committees about actual and potential issues that threaten a professional working relationship. Putting off personnel issues to avoid temporary unpleasantness rarely solves the problems, more often than not, it exacerbates them.
- Treat them professionally and courteously.
- Do not speak ill of them in public, ever.
- If you supervise them, hold them accountable to clear expectations and written guidelines (document incidents and performance related conversations).
- Every once in a while ask yourself, "How am I contributing to this problem?"
- If you supervise them give yourself permission to let them go if it is within your authority; do not delay the process if the staff member shows no sign of being willing to change. Every time I've had to let go of someone, they've thanked me. One person went so far as to say, "What took you so long?"

[1]Carl Rogers, *Client-centered Therapy: Its Current Practice, Implications and Theory* (London: Constable, 1951).

The Ten Best Ways to Ruin Your Staff

For those pastoral leaders who want to keep and develop quality ministry staff colleagues, here are the ten most common ways pastors ruin church staff—and how to avoid them. (For those pastors who *want* to get rid of troubling church staff, then this is the way to do it!).

1. **Demand perfection and conformity.** Insecure leaders tend to demand unrealistic expectations. If you are a secure leader, however, you will seek out mature and competent staff and free them to work out their ministry. You will learn from them—they will be good teachers to you, challenge you, and be colleagues in ministry (I often tell associate staff that "Job 1" of any staff specialist—education, youth, worship, music—is to educate the pastor). If you get a novice staff member, then remember that you'll be doing a lot of on-the-job training. Part of your ministry then, is to be a mentor. That's a call to stewardship related to the profession.

Let your staff make their own mistakes and remember that their mistakes and failures along the way are not a reflection on you. Pastoral ministry is not science, it is relationship. Staff relationships take a long time to cultivate and along the way, it will be messy.

2. **Micromanage and overfunction.** Insecure leaders tend toward being willful and lack an ability to respect boundaries. Those tendencies manifest themselves in overfunctioning, herding and groupthink. Overfunctioning leaders take responsibility for what is not theirs. They take on others' anxiety and impose themselves on their staff: micromanaging their work, setting their schedules, and thinking for them. For example, they'll ask how many were in attendance at Sunday School (then offer pointed suggestions for increasing attendance), insist on unrealistic office hours, set program goals for staff members (often without the staff member's consultation), or, make staff members responsible for other people's functioning.

Effective leaders treat their staff like professionals, knowing that staff will rise to the leader's level of expectations, but more importantly, they will rise to the level of the example the leader sets. Effective leaders allow their staff to shape their ministry—it's what they were called to do.

3. **Divide and conquer.** Insecure leaders tend to play a game of divide and conquer with their staff. Fearful of losing control or influence they are not able to develop their staff into a team of colleagues. They engage in secrecy, sharing information with some individuals on staff while withholding it from others. The result is that staff members never really know what's going on and become perpetually territorial. Effective leaders realize that specialization does not mean compartmentalization. The best staff members are team players and they understand that the ministry belongs to all of them together, not separately. Effective pastoral leaders work at cultivating a team of ministry colleague by developing trust through honesty. They appreciate that a strong staff team is their primary resource for ministry leadership.

4. **Neglect a theology of calling.** A key question for a theology of calling is, "Does the church call the staff, or does the pastor "hire" the staff?" Answer the question one way and staff "belongs to the pastor." Answer another way and it reframes the staff's relationship with the congregation and its members. Insecure pastors will have a tendency to get in the way of staff members' relationship with the church. This puts them in a perpetual triangle between staff members and the congregation. The triangulated dynamic is the same, though the behavior takes many forms: protecting staff from congregation or vise-versa; limiting access to church members (one pastor did not permit

pastoral or program staff to visit church members in the hospital); keeping staff and church leaders at a distance from each other (one pastor did not allow the personnel committee to meet with staff unless he was present); or playing "let's you and them fight" with staff and congregational members or committees.

Secure pastoral leaders foster a theology of calling in their congregations. They allow the church to call and take ownership of their staff. And they allow staff members to work out their relationships with the congregation.

5. **Do not plan corporate worship together.** There is no better way to isolate staff members and fail to develop a shared staff culture than to fail to do weekly worship planning together. I remain amazed at the number of pastoral leaders who do worship planning in isolation, or, assign it as a task to a specialist staff member.

There are few ways as meaningful and effective for developing a strong staff than to plan the weekly worship service together. Here are some of the benefits of doing so:

- It provides an opportunity for staff members to spend time together
- It cultivates a shared corporate theology of church and worship
- It provides opportunity for the spiritual disciplines of prayer, theological reflection, and confession
- It cultivates ownership in the single most important practice of the church: corporate worship
- It taps into the talent and expertise that each staff member can contribute to shaping the central activity of the congregation
- It helps foster the development of a staff culture, with shared values, perspectives, and practices.

Here are two additional insights:

1. Staff members' participation in leading worship validates their ministry in the eyes of the congregation. Most program staff persons work in the background. Therefore, most congregational members have little idea about what their church staff do on a daily basis, or, how their ministry contributes to the church's life and work. Giving opportunity to staff members for providing "pastoral leadership" through corporate worship goes a long way in validating their ministry for those members outside their sphere of influence. Staff worship leadership is received as no small recognition by the church members that the pastor affirms the staff's ministry.

2. The amount of time, thought, and attention you give to worship planning is evident to your church members. We can tell the difference between a theologically-informed worship service and something put together out of routine and habit. After moving into a new town our family was looking for a church to join. At the conclusion of a Sunday worship service at one church my youngest son, then a teenager, commented, "I guess they didn't have time to do worship planning this week." That just to say that even a teenager can discern how much effort and thought goes into worship planning. Needless to say, we never returned to that congregation.

6. **Maintain a dysfunctional personnel committee.** Most congregations of a certain size have a personnel committee, church-staff committee, staff parish relations committee, or a variation of the sort. And, in most congregations, that committee tends to be the most underfunctioning and ineffective committee. There are many causes for it, including the fact that laypersons

often feel inadequate, and therefore reluctant, in critiquing the work of the clergy. When it comes to staff persons, most church members have little understanding of what their work entails. Another factor, however, is that pastors spend too little time investing in that committee and developing it into an asset for the congregation and its staff.

The result is staff and personnel issues are neglected until they become a crisis of enough proportion that resolution of the matter becomes impossible. It is akin to the complaint of ministers that by the time a couple in church come to them for marital counseling, the decision to separate has already been made. Other consequences are a lack of staff performance review and development, and, a failure to acknowledge and celebrate the good work and accomplishments of staff. In many cases a pastor's failure to cultivate a highly functioning personnel committee results in tolerating mediocrity in staff members.

Effective pastoral leaders cultivate the resources that foster health and responsibility in the congregation, and the personnel committee can be one of those. That group can challenge their congregations to hold its pastoral staff accountable, and it can encourage all who are called to serve to aim for high standards.

7. **Make staff members responsible for other people's functioning.** A sure sign of reactivity and anxiety is when pastoral leaders start making staff members responsible for the functioning or behavior of others. One of the things that most frequently brings staff members to a coaching session with me is when the pastor has triangled them in this manner. For example, a church educator is pressured to increase the number of people attending educational programs; a youth minister is held accountable for the

behavior of the church youth; a staff member on the stewardship committee is held responsible for the shortfall in budget giving; a children's minister is held responsible for the spiritual decisions of the children in the church (read: getting them baptized).

Effective leaders understand that staff members are responsible for the stewardship of their ministry, not for the decisions or functioning of the members in the church.

8. **Lower your expectations and your standards.** I am constantly taken aback at the low expectations congregations, and their pastors, seem to hold for their staff members. Too many congregations seem to have the mentality that they do not deserve, or are unable, to get the best persons out there. So, they take the attitude of "settling" for whomever they get. At my last congregation one constant message I received over six years, meant as a compliment, was, "We know we can't keep you." Repeated often enough, that kind of compliment becomes a self-fulfilling prophecy.

Effective pastoral leaders cultivate the perspective that their congregations deserve the best, and therefore, they choose the best staff. Their church deserves it, they deserve it, and, the kingdom of God deserves it. There is no valid reason for settling for and tolerating mediocrity in church staff. If you accept lower standards and tolerate mediocre performance from staff, you'll lose your best people first. That said, here are some things to keep in mind:

- Experience counts (most of the time), but personal maturity counts for more. When seeking good staff, I'd choose personal maturity over experience almost every time.
- Invest in the long-term (it takes three years to get competent at any job; five years to develop a program; six years to get

settled; eight years to be fully accepted by the congregation). A string of short-termed staff tenures gets you nowhere.

- Pastors who set high standards for their staff members need to function at a high level of competence and professionalism themselves. There are fewer ways to lose the respect of your staff than to be a poor performer and unprofessional. Set your own standards, but set them high.

9. **Neglect your own spiritual and personal growth**. You can only influence your staff to be spiritual leaders to your congregation to the extent that YOU are growing in your own spiritual life. Congregations love overfunctioning staff, they do not mind asking staff to sacrifice their families and health on the altar of the church. The pastoral leader must set the example for stewardship of one's vocation and personal life. Modeling ways to invest in your own personal and spiritual growth, professional development, and self care can empower your staff to follow suit.

Additionally, here are three facts that pastoral leaders often forget related to neglecting their own care and needs:

1. When you don't study, we can tell.
2. When you're not spiritually centered, we can tell.
3. When you don't feed yourself, we starve.

It took me ten years after I graduated seminary to find my first church position. One factor was my determination to only accept a ministry position that was a good "fit." The second was that it took me that long to find a pastor who gave evidence that he was still working on his personal growth. In the course of ten years interviewing with congregations and their pastors I had not met one pastor who gave evidence of personal growth over time, participated regularly in professional development, or was able to articulate plans or activities related to a commitment to personal and spiritual growth. The stewardship of ministry, and of one's life, is key to effective pastoral leadership.

10. **Do not invest in your staff's professional development.** Developing a good staff does not come about by happenstance. A collegial staff relationship can be one of the most sustaining and gratifying aspects of congregational ministry. The reality is the pastoral leader needs to be intentional about what kind of staff he or she desires to eventually have. That requires investing in the cultivation of a good staff, including:

- Challenge your church to develop a vision for staff (team) development
- Put money in the budget for staff development, and don't let it be the first thing to cut when there's a budget crisis
- Invest in your own professional development, it sets the example for both congregation and staff
- Develop a sabbatical leave program or policy. Require of staff professional development plans.
- Read together as a staff.

Which relationships feed and challenge you in your pastoral ministry? Your relationship with your staff should be one.

Finally, here is what church staff members say are the ways pastors can cultivate and keep a good staff:

- Provide challenge (vision, courage). Develop a staff culture based on shared values of excellence, commitment, responsibility and mutual accountability. Expect and demand evidence of growth, spiritual, personal, and professional, over the course of time together.

- Be the Resident Theologian. Get your theology of church straight, then, cultivate a common, shared theology among all key persons in the congregation
- Be an enabler, which is helping your staff find and work out their calling in your congregation
- Be a Team Leader. You are responsible for the creation and maintenance of an effective team, and, the culture that fosters it
- Be a Servant Leader. Be redemptive in your relationship with staff, and, model what it means to be a servant leader.
- Be a Primary Educator. This includes being a learner, investing in regular continuing education, taking your sabbatical, encouraging your staff to do likewise
- Always support your staff. Value their vision and their plans. Allow them to craft and shape the ministry they were called to.
- Have a pastoral spirit toward your staff. They are your colleagues, not your "hires." Some pastors even avoid using the term "My staff" to clarify that the staff belongs to the church, not to them.
- Protect them from the willful and destructive people in your congregation. In the long run, pastors do well to be less fearful about losing a few troubling church members than about losing good staff.
- Never ask your staff to do things you are not willing to do yourself. And never, ever, take credit for their work.

The Myth of Fairness

Most of us carry a little tape in our heads of things our mothers said repeatedly. Sometimes we repeat those things, often unintentionally mimicking mom's voice. One of those things your mother probably said, especially if you had siblings, or, when little friends came over to play was, "Play fair!" But you likely remember what your mother also said on those occasions you protested "It's not fair!" She likely quipped, as countless mothers have through the ages, "Life's not fair." (And, if your mother was like mine, she may have added, "Get over it.").

One source of anxiety for many leaders is the need to be, or at least appear to be, "fair." Adult employees or staff persons, like children, will cry "foul" when they feel they are treated unfairly. Reactive employees, or church members, will be quick to charge pastoral leaders with being unfair as a quick way to get a hearing or an advantage. The trap for the leader comes when he or she feels the need to live up to the expectation that it is the leader's job to always be fair, and to live up to whatever that means for everybody in the system.

However, the fact is, as your mother said, life is not fair. Further, not everything is equitable or needs to be. What seems fair to one person or group in the system will seem unfair to another. While I always say "Never question people's motives," I am also fond of reminding myself, "Never underestimate the power of the baser motivations." On any given day, anxious persons will always choose what is best for them over what is best for the system.

Recently a pastor shared his experience during a church business meeting at which a troubling and willful church member took the floor during a time of debate. As is typical during times of congregational crises, attendance during this particular business meeting was robust. Acting as moderator the pastor sought to keep things orderly and announced that each person would be allowed to speak three minutes for or against the issue under debate. The troubling member was the first to stand to have his say, but strongly protested that three minutes was not enough time to speak his case.

Not wishing to seem unfair, and thereby antagonizing the troubling member and his supporters, the pastor said that he would stick to the three minute rule, but would allow others to "give" the speaker their three minutes. Whereupon, starting with the man's daughter, several people "gave" the man their three minutes, enabling him to go on to monopolize the business meeting for about fifteen minutes!

In a moment full of anxiety, trying to appear "fair" (and likely with all good intentions about acting fairly) this leader effectively not only empowered the most willful person in the room, but also failed to challenge people to take personal responsibility for their thoughts and beliefs. The tactic failed to challenge persons to take a self-defining stance for their positions, viewpoints, or beliefs. Instead, this leader facilitated a "herding" mentality. Instead of each individual standing up and taking responsibility for him- or herself, many chose to allow another to speak for them.

Leadership requires courage, and acting courageously in the midst of crisis is hard. But leaders need to remember that they are first responsible for the welfare and health of the system as a whole, and their own functioning in their leader position. Everything else is secondary: other people's functioning, other people's happiness, or, whether every decision is "fair" for every individual or group in the system.

❖

Possibility and Potentiality

I had an interesting conversation with a local church minister who expressed frustration about his congregation's failure to live fully into its possibility. That's not an uncommon frustration for pastors and local church leaders. But I have found it helpful to make a distinction between possibility and potentiality, between what is theoretically possible and what is potentially viable.

In my thinking possibility refers to a future prospect. In a sense, to say "anything is possible" can be true, within reason. A congregation that is in its establishment phase has open-ended possibilities. That translates into an almost palpable sense of hopefulness, lots of energy, and a sense of adventure which facilitate risk-taking. But it does not take long for a new church start to move into its next life stage of formation and formatting.[1] At that point potentiality overshadows possibility. Potentiality has to do with the inherent ability or capacity for growth, development, and agency. While all congregations may be equal at their inception in terms of possibilities, very quickly the reality of their potential becomes evident. Not all congregations have equal potential. The numbers of factors that influence potentiality are numerous: location, culture (values and practices), socio-economic and educational level of members, the capacities of its leaders, social and economic context, etc. Here are some things to keep in mind:

- Some factors related to potentiality are difficult to quantify (like values, attitudes, willingness)
- Some factors may be outside of the control of the congregation (context, location, economics)

- Potentiality may not be related to effectiveness. Some congregations don't grow or develop because they've reached the stage (or conditions) where they are effective enough for their needs and desires.
- Potentiality requires capacity—in other words, "the talent must be in the room."

Distinguishing between the ideals of possibilities and the realities of potentiality may at least get us unhooked from unrealistic expectations.

[1]See Galindo, *The Hidden Lives of Congregations* for a fuller treatment on congregational lifespan stages.

Imaginative Gridlock

I worked with a couple of organizations that were "stuck" but motivated enough to get moving toward becoming "healthier." As I worked with the leaders and employees of both organizations I was reminded of some fundamental truths about systems. First, while motivation is a necessary component for bringing about change, it is not sufficient. For example, if the motivation is to simply ease acute anxiety or pain a system will settle on pragmatic "instant" solutions that will simply ease the symptoms. Once the pain (the symptom) eases, the temptation is to ignore working on the fundamental issues that will move the system toward health. That's logical since working toward health often brings about more, or different, "pain." Any system that lacks tolerance for pain will always settle on being medicated rather than go the "no pain, no gain" route.

Second, the role and the function of the leader are key. I've witnessed two common leadership liabilities in these organizations. In one, the leader had a pattern of adapting to weakness. Specifically, rather than moving toward the most mature persons in the system by soliciting their input and giving them permission to act, the leader tended to give over-attention to the most fearful, anxious, and needy in the system, in that case, it was a group of persons who self-identified as "victims" seeking "protection" and "privileges." The natural tendency of that group to "herd" and "glom together" was perceived by the leader as a "voting block," when in fact, it was the leader's coddling and over-attention to the "needs" and feelings of this group that empowered them.

In the other, the leader lacked an appreciation for the tenacity of the destructive forces in the system, and failed to appreciate the necessary corrective function that the leader must provide, namely, to inhibit the capacity of those forces to sabotage progress toward a vision. Admittedly this is tough since those "forces" often are manifested in the form of personalities in the organization.

Third, both organizations exhibited what Edwin H. Friedman called "Imaginative Gridlock." Friedman identified three characteristics of imaginative gridlock:[1]

The Treadmill Effect. Both organizations were very busy doing the same things and following the same procedures they had been doing for years, and, which had gotten then stuck. Yet they seemed to have an inability to get off the treadmill. Breaking patterns of behaviors and practice proved to be a huge challenge to both organizations. It seems it was just easier to run in place and get nowhere than to get off the treadmill, change their ways, and make progress.

A focus on answers. It's always amazing how quickly the call for answers comes when acute anxiety is present. In one organization this happened in the first meeting! They weren't interested in exploring what the *problem* may be or what their part in it was. They wanted to know not only what I was going to do, but how I was going to do whatever it was that would help them get out of their stuckness (I jokingly had to remind them that a consultant doesn't actually "do" anything).

In the second organization one person kept pushing for "data." That's a sure sign of imaginative gridlock: an inability to move toward adventure, vision, and imagination rather than a search for certitude. When certitude is your highest value, boldness goes out the window as a resource. The fact is that innovators, visionaries, and trendsetters don't work off of "data." They move on imagination fueled by vision.

The polarization of false dichotomies. The third characteristic of imaginative gridlock is "either-or thinking." When the mind is anxious it cannot be imaginative. It tends, therefore, to create false dichotomies and to polarize concepts, options, and opinions. It doesn't take long to begin labeling and personalizing issues, leading to an inability to listen and dialogue. In one organization the result was the formation of "factions" or "camps." Once someone became associated with a "camp" his or her opinions and thoughts were always discounted by another faction—regardless of the merit of the content, opinion, or argument.

Change comes hard to organizations, but even harder to systems that suffer from imaginative gridlock. In these cases it is necessary to focus on changing the way the culture thinks. As Einstein said, "Problems cannot be solved at the same level of awareness that created them."

[1]See Edwin H. Friedman, *A Failure of Nerve* (New York: Church Publishing, Inc., 2007), p. 29ff.

❖

On Ideology:
Two Sides of the Same Coin

Elections can provide endless entertainment, if you're into that sort of thing. There's enough drama at all levels to provide a source of amusement for most people, not the least of which is to watch ideologues in action. Liberals and conservatives (political and religious) tend to provide the steadiest source of amusement, and irk, if only because both camps seem to take themselves so seriously. When they take to the extremes, despite the content of their messages, they become two sides of the same coin.

Some time after I put up my consultation website I received an e-mail from a woman who commented, rather nastily, and at length, on how she would never call on us for a consultation because the only persons on the web page were white males. I responded that (1) I was Hispanic (a non-white minority), (2) there's a word for people who judge others on the basis of their race, skin color, or other secondary characteristic rather than on their character or their performance, (3) the lack of female consultants wasn't for lack of trying; every one we invited had their reasons for not being able to participate as much as they'd wanted to, and, (4) what made her think I cared what she thought?

But, such is the nature of ideologists, they impose their views and values on others and insist on being acknowledged and having their views affirmed. Ideology is a form of non-thinking and can be a veneer for the pseudo-self. Like the person who becoming so steeped in a "12-step" culture as to work only from that frame of reference is forever a victim, forever recovering, perpetually dependent on outside sources of strength of will. I celebrate the success of twelve step recovery programs in helping people cope, but it's the liability of staying stuck in a perpetually dependent and powerless state that is a risk. Ideology can result in rigidity and a lack of tolerance for others' self-definition and points of views.

What characterizes ideology is its willfulness. And, it is willfulness that does the harm in relationships and systems. I've seen this played out in many congregations related to the issue of homosexuality. How does one church escape reactivity related to gays in the church, while another can make it work? Consistently, those congregations that are able to deal with the issue responsibly and with the least level of crisis, reactivity, and toxicity are those in which there is a lack of insistence on conformity (herding) from all camps, the ability to tolerate self-defining stances, and the role of a mediating leader. In all cases I've observed, the leader has been able to function in a highly self-differentiated manner: being clear about where he or she stands (self-defining) while, (1) allowing others to do so, (2) not being willful in insisting on conformity, and (3) allowing the congregation to struggle with the issue while insisting on decency and maturity (and dealing with the willful persons as appropriate). Here's the insight: *the principles are the same regardless of the content of the issue.*

Ideologies can be powerful forces because they can function as a form of idolatry. By that I mean that they exhibit some common characteristics:

- They contain a comprehensive assumption about human experience, thoughts, and the external world (they have an explanation for everything).
- Because ideologies are internally logically consistent, rigid, and coherent it becomes difficult to engage in dialogue. At the end of the day, you can't reason with it.
- They set out a program of social, relational, and political organization in generalized and abstract terms, but offer few pragmatic solutions.
- Their only repertoire for realizing this program entails a polarizing struggle: us against them, and it's only win-or-lose.
- They seek not merely to persuade others on the merit of their belief, but to recruit adherents, demanding a commitment of loyalty.
- They try to impose their views on a wide public but will tend to confer some special role of leadership on intellectuals, victims, or other category of persons.

Jean Bethke Elshtain wrote, *Ideology, by which I mean a totalizing and closed system that discounts or dismisses whatever does not "fit" within it, has very little use for accurate descriptions of what is going on.*[1] Regardless of the content of the ideology, liberal, fundamentalist, conservative, religious, political, etc., the main purpose becomes to offer change through a normative thought process (the one perspective on what the world *ought* to be). Ideologies tend to be abstract ideals applied to reality and, thus, rarely pragmatic.

[1]Jean Bethke Elshtain, *Just War Against Terror: The Burden of American Power in an Unjust World* (New York: Basic Books), p. 16.

The Pastor's Function as Coach

I am often surprised at the disconnect we clergy have from our congregations in several areas. One I see especially seems counterintuitive. We go to conferences to feed our own growth in spirituality and faith, and then fail to share those very things with our congregations. It seems that we somehow assume that the faith of our congregants, and the ways it needs to be nurtured, is somehow different from ours. Similarly, we get coaching to help us gain perspective, learn, and function better, and then we don't see the connection that we should do likewise with our congregational leaders.

During a consultation with a pastor I recommended that he function as a coach to the elders in the church, who were the most mature and non-reactive persons in the system in the midst of a crisis. He said that he'd never thought about functioning in that capacity for his congregational leaders, even though he himself had for years sought out coaching to help him function better.

Following these basic systems principles can make for a productive experiment in learning to function as coach to our congregations:

- The leader is the regulator for health in the system. Therefore, he or she invests in the most mature persons in the system, those capable of learning, growing, and changing their ways of functioning
- The leader solicits health and maturity through challenge. When you issue a challenge, those who can be assets to the system will step up (and those who are either benign or liabilities are quickly identified)
- Work with, and invest in, the most motivated. Trying to get people to change can tip us into a willful posture. Willfulness is what does the harm in any system and is the quickest route to getting stuck or triggering reactivity.
- The leader as coach shares information and educates. This helps provide perspective, foster imagination, and facilitates shifts in patterns of thinking.

Sometimes leaders need to do two things at the same time: containing the pathogens while cultivating the strengths and resources for health of the system. Edwin H. Friedman has good material on the leader as coach in *Generation to Generation*.[1] I address that concept in the book *The Hidden Lives of Congregations* in chapters 8 to 10. And on page 196 there is a section titled "Focus on Coaching and Consulting" that describes this aspect of pastoral leadership.[2]

1Edwin Friedman, *Generation to Generation: Family Process in Church and Synagogue* (New York: The Guilford Press, 1985).

[2]Israel Galindo, *The Hidden Lives of Congregations* (Herndon: The Alban Institute, 2004).

It Only Takes a Few of Them

The forced termination of clergy remains one of the most difficult, and often tragic, issues for congregations. A congregation can take years to recover from the forced termination of a pastor—and so, also, for the pastor. A single episode can become a nodal event that shapes a congregation's culture for years. A series of them can put a congregation on the downslide toward dysfunction or extinction. When a congregation gets a reputation for "eating up clergy" they'll tend to have difficulty attracting mature pastoral leaders, the very kind who can get them back on the road toward health and relevance.

Here's the little secret about forced terminations in the congregational setting we often fail to appreciate: it only takes a few members to tip a crisis toward the forced termination of the pastor. According to a survey, in the majority of cases (60%) the driving force behind a pastoral exit is a small faction who are willful and persistent.

According to the survey, *the vast majority forced out by a faction were forced out by small factions of 10 or less. Although the size of the churches were almost equally divided between those less than and those more than 100 attendees, most of the forced out pastors were driven out by a fraction of the regular worshippers.*[1]

How do a small few get to determine the outcome for the majority? It is not uncommon to hear congregational members express surprise and ignorance about a crisis between the pastor and this small group after the fact. "Why did the pastor leave?" "I was not aware there was a problem." "I thought things were going just fine."

Here are some thoughts on the issue:

- Too many pastors hunker down in isolation when under attack and therefore fail to tap into the resources of the healthier and less reactive members
- Too many pastors fail to take on the issue early and up front, hoping that it will just go away
- Often the faction (as small as ten people) rally around one energized and reactive member who becomes the leader around which reactivity gathers
- Often the presenting issues and the reasons given for the discontent with the pastor has little to do with the pastor
- Pastors and church leaders often fail to appreciate the level of reactivity within the faction, and, the level of tenacity and willfulness they can muster
- Too many church leaders fail by having an "unreasonable faith in reasonableness" when dealing with reactive factions
- Too many pastors, especially young and inexperienced clergy, will take the crisis personally, believing that it is about their character, calling, or competence, when in fact, it is rarely about them aside from the fact that they just happen to be the leader
- Clergy and congregations who value peace at any price will never be able to provide the corrective necessary to deal with factions
- Ultimately dealing with these factions will be a test of courage for pastors and congregational leaders called to deal with the crisis.

A great resource for clergy and congregations dealing with issues of forced termination is the Ministering to Ministers Foundation. Contact their executive director, Charles Chandler at: www.mtmfoundation.org.

[1]S. Barfoot, B, Winston, and C. Wickman,"Forced Pastoral Exits: An Exploratory Study," Regent University's School of Global Leadership & Entrepreneurship Working Paper (2004): 5.

Are Humans A "Pack Animal"?

After a long period of deliberation I finally got around to doing a presentation on "Leadership Lessons from the Dog Whisperer" for a group of clergy. It was a fun presentation and seemed well-received. As often happens in presentations participants focused on the metaphor as a frame of reference for discussions. It was amusing to hear how many dog references were made during the course of the conference.

I started the presentation by framing my playful approach in using the dog whisperer as a corollary to thinking about leadership in congregations from a systems perspective.

One participant, in his struggle to decide to what extent a corollary can be stretched to an equivalence, asked, "Are people 'pack animals' in the same way as canines?"

Corollary – n. (logic).
1. A proposition that follows with little or no proof required from one already proven.
2. A deduction or an inference.
3. The reasoning involved in drawing a conclusion or making a logical judgment on the basis of circumstantial evidence and prior conclusions rather than on the basis of direct observation.

I responded that perhaps, yes, people are "pack animals" biologically, if only in the sense that we constantly struggle with the togetherness-separateness forces in emotional relationship systems, being an individual while remaining part of the group. Our cortex is what moves us toward individuation (Yeah, yeah, pure "Bowenians" don't like the term individuation, but that doesn't change the fact of it). People are "social beings." There is no self apart from community, and thereby is the tension between individuation and togetherness. Therein is the frame of reference for self-differentiation: being an individual self without cutting off from the social relationships of one's system that also defines who one is.

But I have also observed that in times of anxiety, when the cortex is not a resource to the self (that resides in the mid-brain), people "herd." They become a "pack" (we sometimes call it a "mob") and will rally around *any* "pack leader"—often the person who is, or is perceived as, most "dominant." As Millan, the dog whisperer, points out, that dominant person can be dysfunctional, but when anxiety triggers "herding" there's nothing logical about it—it is just reactivity. It is often the case that anxious, reactive, non-differentiated people will become a "pack" around any person perceived as leader.

At one point in the conversation the participant said, *Speaking theoretically, is the human togetherness force the same as the "pack animal" force? I don't think so. I think the presence of the cortex changes everything. There is still the togetherness force (necessary for the preservation of life, etc.), but the possibility of intentional attention to and cooperation with the individual force introduces a basic difference. Thinking theologically, this leads to my understanding of God's intent in creation—the creation of beings capable of relationship with the Creator. Is this a reality without the cooperation (faith response) of the human?*

Perhaps not. Is this the chief way we are co-creators? At this point in my pilgrimage, I believe it is.

Bowen family systems theory challenges us to consider how our biology defines us as humans as much as, or more than, the assumptions we hold about the impact and influence of our cognition. It keeps the interesting question about nature vs. nurture alive and well, and refreshingly interesting.

Process vs. Procedure

Some years ago one of my boys worked for hours on a work of art on a computer graphics program. When he tried to print out his masterpiece, however, the color printer spewed out a monochrome facsimile of his creation, very different from how it appeared on the computer screen. Apparently, the ink had run out in my color printer's ink cartridge. Well, I knew what I had to do, change the ink cartridge. I understood the process: remove the old cartridge and replace it with a new one, which I did. Unfortunately the only reward I got for my trouble was blinking error lights all over the place. The computer flashed an error message telling me the printer wasn't working (Thanks. Tell me something I don't know!), and more flashing lights on the printer itself indicating something was wrong, but not telling me exactly what.

I tried removing the cartridge and replacing it again. Turned the printer on and off several times, hit the reset button, and anything else I could think of. Nothing worked. Finally, I pulled out the owner's manual and, feeling like a dummy, followed the printer cartridge replacement instructions step by step. Lo and behold, it worked! My problem was that while I understood the process, I had not followed the right procedure.

I'm hearing a lot of talk about process these days. In a way, that's welcomed. It used to be that I seemed to be one of the few proponents for it in the "process vs. product" debate. On the other hand, like many concepts that trickle down into popular vernacular, the meaning of the term *process* may become lost in the quagmire of the fuzzy thinking that comes from overuse and over-familiarity. We lose a lot of good words (and ideas) that way. Remember the word paradigm? Good word. Good concept. But we've lost it due to overuse. I've even heard one person cringe, "If I hear the word 'paradigm' one more time I'm going to scream!"

A hint that this may have already happened with process is its current confusion with the term "procedure." It is a not-too-subtle distinction, yet the terms often are used interchangeably. And now I am the one who cringes and feels like screaming, "Process is NOT procedure!"

The dictionary defines process as "a continuing development involving many changes." Procedure is defined as "a particular course of action or way of doing something; the established way of carrying on the business."

There's a subtle but important difference there. To miss it can lead us astray in accomplishing what we need. In teaching, as in many areas, you can fail by understanding the process but not following the procedure. More often than not, however, we follow procedure and mistakenly believe we are giving attention to process. For example, a good teacher understands the teaching-learning process and creates the appropriate procedure for making it happen consistent to the goal at hand. A poor teacher will become a slave to procedure because he or she fails to understand the dynamic process of the art of teaching and the dynamics of learning. Too often, we believe that in creating and following procedures we allow the necessary processes to take place. In the end, you can take all the right steps, and still get it wrong!

Process n. *A continuing development involving many changes.*

Procedure n. *1.A particular course of action or way of doing something 2.The established way of carrying on the business.*

The key to understanding the distinction between these two terms is found in a phrase in the definition given above. In process, we give attention to a continuing development involving many changes, which, hints that while procedure is predictable, process is not. Process has to do with the flowing dynamics and forces at play in any endeavor. It leaves room for the unpredictable. It respects the serendipity of un-factored data, hidden agendas, mysterious forces, queer cosmic convergences, and Murphy's Law, which says that in any given endeavor, anything that can possibly go wrong, will!

A proper understanding of process helps us see below the surface of the deceptive orderly appearances of lesson plans, timelines, strategic plans, and Gant charts. It accepts that in any endeavor we must be open to changes and challenges because of the unpredictable nature of things which are in a state of continuing development. But we can say, "trust the process" because the process will bring us where we need to be—even when we're not quite sure of where we'll end up. In my experience, it is the process that gets you there, not procedure. This shouldn't surprise us too much; it is a great theological concept. Trust the Spirit, we say, when we've run out of plans or there are no procedures to follow. "It's the journey, not the destination," we are reminded.

Procedure can tell us how to pack the bags, but it's the process that lets us make the journey in a spirit of adventure. Procedure is helpful, even necessary. But it is just a tool, and tools can become obsolete in the middle of a project that is ever changing, ever evolving, ever growing. Paying attention to process will allow us to switch tools when needed.

Good Leaders Don't Motivate

I continue to come across the idea that it is the job of leaders to motivate others. I'm becoming convinced that is a wrong notion. I think it is fine that people "get motivated" out of their internal, intrinsic, agency. In fact, few things get done without motivation, but I think it is a risky notion to believe that it is the responsibility of the leader in any organization to motivate others to action. That runs the risk of quickly tipping into the manipulative if not, ultimately, the willful—through coercion (manipulation), seduction (charm), or inappropriate influence (power). It is worth remembering that, regardless of intentions, it is willfulness that does the harm.

However, I do think that what a good leader does is inspire others. The difference is that motivation influenced by the leader is external to the person. It is an intentional attempt to move another toward an action or goal held by, or desired by, the leader. Inspiration, on the other hand, is a dynamic that addresses the self. A leader that inspires me draws something from within me. He or she taps into something within my authentic self in a way that resonates with my own values, goals, and desires. Inspiration taps into the intrinsic agency of my own self-direction.

When a leader inspires he or she communicates from the stance of challenge and invitation whose source is the leader's own self. Attempts at motivating others, however, strike me as too close to external manipulation toward action. Ultimately that is ineffective because external motivation has a very short shelf life. I think both, motivation and inspiration, are resources available to any leader. Let's just confess that motivating others is relatively easy to do and therefore, convenient. Anyone with a modicum of knowledge about stimulus-response dynamics or simple psychology can get someone to do something—whether they like it or not or want to or not. In fact, there is no quicker way to motivate someone than to appeal to the baser motivations, but I think that in the long run, for cultivating a healthier system, inspiration is a more worthy function and orientation for the leader. Are you an inspiring leader?

Leaving Well

I have had many conversations with clergy who are contemplating leaving their ministry settings. It's not unusual for these consultations to come in waves, and it is always interesting that they do. It seems that issues, crises, and topics have their seasons. I've not yet learned to read the signs in the wind or in the patterns of the clouds to know how to anticipate when that phenomenon happens, I just accept that these things "come in threes" as they say—or fives or sixes.

I have heard from maternity unit nurses that they experience the same phenomenon—things are quiet for a spell and, then, there's a serial population explosion. And when I managed a funeral home it was the same: all quiet for a while and then St. Peter seemed to throw open the Pearly Gates and we'd get a string of calls. I sometimes wondered if there was a correlation between the infant population explosion and the exit of souls from the planet. Somebody ought to do a study on that.

Whether clergy are leaving under duress or because they feel stirrings of restlessness, certain issues seem common to the nature of leaving regardless of the circumstances. Leaving a congregation involves the murky process of discernment, and clarity rarely comes instantly or easily. In many cases I've witnessed clergy who have left their congregations emotionally before they began thinking consciously about leaving. It's not unusual in those cases for the congregation to *sense* it before the pastor *realizes* it.

In most cases the discernment process involves getting clear about what counts as important to factor into the decision and what can be dismissed as inconsequential. In the early stages of discernment that is not easy to do. At those stages everything seems as important as everything else and so the feeling is one of being stuck.

There's no shortcut to the discernment process, primarily because it is as much an emotional process as it is an intellectual one. In fact, in my experience, rationality rarely is of real significance in decisions about staying or leaving, as much as we'd like to believe otherwise. If it were as simple as "doing the math" we wouldn't have as much trouble reaching a point of decision, nor experience as much angst as we do.

While there is no shortcut to discerning whether to leave a congregation, and insight comes in its own time, here are some points of consideration when trying to leave well. These aren't easy, for they are often contrary to how most clergy seem to approach the issue:

Don't plan for the congregation's future. When it's time for you to leave a congregation narrow your vision. Concentrate on leaving well and give the congregation's future to the congregation—that is no longer your responsibility. To be blunt, once you decide to leave, your congregation's future is none of your business.

If you're going to go, go. You don't need to burn your bridges, but you need to get clear about what leaving means. Most clergy seem to do well once they get clear on this point. For example, they will communicate with their congregation that when they leave they are no longer the "pastor." So they'll not make pastoral calls, conduct weddings and funerals, or get involved in church business. Clergy who are not able to "go" (or to let go) tend to become the bane of the new pastors and often do a great disservice to the congregation. It's amazing how many clergy have trouble "leaving" their congregations. Sometimes they try to come back as "members." I've yet to see a former pastor of a congregation able to successfully return to their former congregation as "just a member." It seems hard for them to appreciate that they weren't "just a member" before, and never will be. More often than not, for example, they will be introduced as, "this is our former pastor."

As you are leaving, the function of your preaching needs to change. That change in function is primarily one of a prophetic theological hope. This isn't the time to try to plant insight into your congregation—if they didn't get what you've been trying to say all those years they're certainly not going to "get it" now. They're listening to you differently. What they want to hear, and need to hear, is the affirmation of hope that they'll be just fine without you!

The second function of preaching at this time is to remind them of their story. Clergy often are the resident storytellers of the narrative history of the congregation. Too often a congregation experiences an episode of corporate amnesia when a pastor leaves. Now is the time to tell, and retell, the story of the congregation as a local people of God. Remind them of how they came to be, who they were, and who they are.

Stay connected. One common emotional response of clergy who are leaving is to emotionally defect in place and begin to "disconnect" from their congregation. That's understandable and may be a function of anticipatory grieving. But clergy need to work at staying emotionally connected to significant persons in the congregation, its leaders as well as others worth investing time.

Work on your grieving. Leaving a congregation, under whatever circumstance, involves loss, and loss requires grieving.

Own it. Find ways to mourn appropriately (mourning is the outward expression of grieving), but don't confuse your grieving with that of the congregation. Your congregation will not likely grieve to the same depth, or the same things, as you will.

Focus on your own vision and work on your own self. In the early stages of discernment it is difficult to sift the important from the insignificant. In the midst of the fog of discernment clergy get stuck by considering, with equal weight, issues like, the children (even when they are grown!), the house, their age, the spouse (his or her job, friends, hobbies, etc.), giving up a short commute, the club, the salary, a perk, their nice office, the computer the church provided, etc. To be sure these may be important—but they are not as important as pursuing your own vision, calling, and goals. Change involves risk and it involves loss. As someone said, you can have anything you want, but you cannot have everything you want. The question becomes, "What are you willing to give up in order to pursue your calling, vision, dreams, or passion?"

"There's A Disturbance in the Force."

I like Star Wars, the movie, as much as the next person—at least the original. While not technically sophisticated, or particularly well-acted, nevertheless it retains its charm. During a presentation I misquoted the great Ben Kenobe as saying "There's a disturbance in the force," and was promptly called on my error. There's nothing like being corrected by a 16-year-old Star Wars geek on a quote from a movie I saw during its *original* release. In a movie theater. Before the uppity kid was even born![1]

Like Kenobe, systems can detect when there's a disturbance in the emotional field. In a congregation reactivity from a disturbance in the emotional field can result from:

- The arrival or departure of a significant group of people
- The departure and loss of a significant number of people
- The arrival of a significant number of "different" people
- The departure of a minister who was fused with the system
- The arrival of the new minister
- A change in the physical plant of the congregation
- A change in meeting patterns (especially those related to corporate worship)
- A change in policies that affect people's jobs, ministries, schedules, or relationships
- Changes in the finances of the congregation (increased giving, decreased giving, increased expenses, large gifts for endowments or for designated programs or causes)
- Attempts to change symbols or artifacts related to the congregation's identity or culture
- Shifts in the surrounding community environment
- The discovery of illegal or unethical conduct among clergy or the members.[2]

Disturbances in the emotional field of a relationship system are caused by anything that threatens to change the homeostasis. The reason isn't so much that change is a threat, but that change brings a challenge to the emotional system's corporate identity, its sense of self—and the threat of change in functioning of the individuals that make up the system. These two changes are the cause of anxiety, though the reasons people attribute to the anxiety are varied.

The important thing to remember is that change is the norm, yet it will be resisted due to systemic homeostasis. Most systems with a level of health have the resilience to ride the wave of change and come out on the other side of the chaos-of-the-in-between and arrive at a new equilibrium. But when the normal anxiety that is the by-product of change goes unregulated it can result in reactivity. Wise leaders learn to recognize reactivity of this nature and will know that they must allow for people to work through their anxiety and reactivity *for themselves*, although, not by themselvess. The leader who has a low tolerance for others' anxieties or discomfort often is too quick to move to ease people's existential pain. Often this merely results in self-sabotage and in aborting the change process necessary to come out on the other side of things.

[1]The line was, "I feel a great disturbance in the force," uttered by Obi-Wan Kenobi (It's kind of scary that I actually know that).
[2]Source: Adapted from a handout of a presentation by Betty Pugh Mills. Original source not cited.

That Vision Thing

During a hallway conversation with a former minister who recently took a job in educational administration the topic of the newbie learning curve came up. He unburdened about how, after a year on the job, he was still on a learning curve. I shared with him that I tell seminarians that it takes about three years to become competent at a new job. He laughed and recalled how he had to learn that lesson the hard way in his early pastorates. Now, he says, he tells starting clergy to not do anything for about two years, and after that, to "only take baby steps" when trying to bring about change.

I'm still convinced that clergy can't really do "that vision thing" until they are in their fifth year at their congregations. It just takes that long to get to know the complex matrix of culture, corporate identity, and network of relationships that constitutes a congregation well enough to formulate a vision. I usually get two responses to that statement: (1) a shake of the head saying that is too long, and, (2) a nod that it's about right. Given that vision is a key function of leadership I can understand why leaders are eager to offer it. But offering it during one's first year at a congregation always strikes me as both misinformed and willful.

Vision is important, but it doesn't arise out of thin air. Vision is not something disconnected from other factors, like context, personal and corporate values, relationships, mission or what Stephen J. Trachtenberg, former president of George Washington University called a "point of view." Trachtenberg has an interesting perspective on that vision thing:

Another lesson is about leadership, a simple word that has acquired a peacock tail of complexity trailing behind it. I want to offer just one bright feather. Leadership, *we read in endless management books, requires "vision," so a leader needs to be "a visionary." We shouldn't believe that. Ezekiel was a visionary, and Chapters 1 and 37 of Ezekiel in the Old Testament are moving and some of the finest scriptural eloquence we have. But I doubt that I am alone in being confused about the wheels in Chapter 1 and the dry bones in Chapter 37. Sometimes it is better to be concrete than eloquent. It is better to have a point of view or a series of goals than a vision that is subject to many interpretations or baffled silence.*[1]

That perspective rings true to me, especially if by "point of view" he means something akin to a philosophy or set of guiding principles that facilitate discernment about what is important and what is not, about what is expedient and what is right, or about what is urgent to address and what can wait. And while a vision can inspire, inspiration without perspiration tends to get you nowhere. People may stand and applaud a vision, but concrete goals will get them to roll up their sleeves and get to purposeful work.

[1]Stephen J. Trachtenberg, "Lessons from the Top," *The Chronicle of Higher Education* (Nov. 2, 1007, p. B5).

Do Not Judge

At a conference I experienced that familiar unsettling situation where an audience member asks a question, you do the best you can to respond on your feet in-the-moment, only to later, after the event is over, come up with a really good response. It's that moment when you say to yourself, "Darn! I wish I'd said that then."

There seems to have been an issue with this particular group of folks related to "judging." A previous speaker was challenged on a comment by someone in that audience who said, "It sounds like you're judging." This was a similar response to a comment I'd made. My response to the audience member was, "Sounds like you have a problem with judging. Tell me more."

The fact that the audience chuckled was a clue to me that indeed, this crowd seemed to have an issue with "judging."

What I wish I'd said then is: there's a difference between being judgmental and exercising good judgment. Being judgmental is a myopic and prejudicial attitude that inhibits dialogue, insight, and does not allow for a self-differentiated position. But I don't know how a leader can be effective without practicing good judgment, or, judging. It is, perhaps, what we refer to in religious language as "discernment." A good leader is constantly having to make a judgment between one thing and another, and, sometimes, between one person and another. For example, when you need to make a new hire and you have to judge the best qualified among a dozen applicants. We rarely make a hire based on the 'most qualified,' rather, on the basis of who we judge to be *the best fit*. The leader in any system is required to practice judgment—choosing based on clarity of one's rationale. Lacking the capacity to practice good judgment one is left victim to uncertainty, whims, and predilections.

Sound judgment requires clarity about one's values, beliefs, and a commitment to the informing principles that guide us. Those are the same things necessary to practice self-definition and for self-differentiation.

I'm not sure about the source of the inspeak about "judging is bad" in that group I addressed. But it seems to me that it may be a case of misunderstanding and fuzzy thinking. That often happens when dealing with terms with common roots, like "judgment" and "judgmental." The problem with misunderstanding, and the reason it is important to provide a corrective, is that misunderstanding leads to misapplication.

Common Sense in Pastoral Leadership

Emotional Intelligence is one of the fields of research that currently is being applied to pastoral leadership. I think it holds great promise for effective pastoral leadership because the nature of leadership in the (systemic) context of congregations is more about understanding emotional fields than about anything else typically associated with what constitutes leadership (e.g., management skills, education, intellect, good looks, personality style, etc.). But I think in many cases, common sense may be as valuable an asset for the leaders as a high score on any emotional intelligence inventory.

Here are some common sense practices too many congregational leaders, whether pastors or staff, neglect:

- Visit in the homes of your members
- Accept people where they are on the journey of faith
- Be sensitive to the problems and realities of "lay" members who live in a secular, *real* world
- Learn when to speak and when to keep your mouth shut
- Be tactful—never embarrass a church member or a child
- Greet people when they are in church
- Never take sides in personal issues between members. Ever.
- Be responsible in keeping confidences, but don't get caught in the "bind of confidentiality"
- Listen to your critics—they are not always 100% wrong
- Apologize when you know you are in the wrong
- Visit your members in the hospital and those who are shut-ins
- Be present with family members when someone in the family is in surgery

- Be a responsible steward of your money—including your financial giving to the church
- As often as possible, express genuine appreciation and encouragement to members and staff.

If those sound rather basic and self-evident it is because they are. Anyone with common sense will do those things. But that's the point: more pastors and staff lose their effectiveness in ministry (and not too few have lost a congregation) by lacking the common sense to *actually do those things.*

How to Run Any Organization

I have a book on my bookshelf titled *How To Run Any Organization,* by Theodore Caplow.[1] The clever title caught my attention and I snatched it up from the used bookstore I frequented during my pecuniary seminary days. I was eager to learn any secrets it could reveal as I was starting my first administrative job. Never having been in a position of primary leadership in any organization I was hoping for a crash course in "how to succeed in business without really trying."

Books and articles that promise to unlock the secrets of success are plentiful. They shamelessly promise insight without the effort of thinking, success with little effort, wisdom without the trial of experience, and winning with no risk. Most of those books are not much more than snake oil in print. And they succeed because snake oil will always sell (heck, I bought the book, didn't I?).

But the better books of this sort are those that address "the fundamentals." They identify the basics about leadership while avoiding the promise of magical solutions, silver bullets, or silly metaphors that substitute for insight. The more responsible authors share genuine insight culled from the experience of failure and of lessons learned in the school of hard knocks. They value excellence over success and find more satisfaction in the practice of integrity than the bottom line.

Culling my files one day I came across an article I'd saved from a 2003 issue of *The Economist* titled, "How to run a company well." The article lists "a ten-point checklist of the necessary qualities" of effective leadership. Here's the list:

1. A sound ethical compass
2. The ability to take [sic] unpleasant decisions
3. Clarity and focus
4. Ambition
5. Effective communication skills
6. The ability to judge people
7. A knack for developing talent
8. Emotional self-confidence
9. Adaptability
10. Charm.

You can read the entire article on the website of The *Economist* magazine. What do you think?

- Is there something missing that you'd add to the list?
- Is there something on the list you don't agree with?
- In the context of congregational leadership, would the list be different? How so?
- Does this list apply to those who occupy "second chair" leadership positions? Is their list different?

[1]Theodore Caplow, *How To Run Any Organization* (New York: The Dryden Press, 1976).

Knowing When To Fold 'Em

Congregational staff who occupy the "second chair" often find themselves in a precarious position related to the prospects of their tenure. Sometimes circumstances dictate this, but also, the relationship with the senior pastor can be a major factor.

One insight that can be of help when both circumstance and relationship make for a prickly situation is that during times of acute anxiety the issue is not about some of the things we assume *should* matter. For example, I've heard church staff members, who are trying to sort out conflict that involves their job (meaning, there's a threat to dismiss the staff person), want to argue on the merit of things like:

- their tenure
- their competence
- their expertise in the field
- their past glowing annual personnel reviews
- their sincerity
- their good service
- the fact that they are "nice persons."

Staff members often are taken aback to discover that none of those tend to count for much, or are given merit, during times of reactivity, if staff become the focus of anxiety (resulting in scapegoating, blame-displacement, or personalization of issues). Reactivity is not about logic and reasonableness. People who are in the throes of reactivity are not interested in dialogue—the bottom line is, they just want their way.

Here's what it sounds like:

"I've been here 10 years. They wouldn't just dismiss me or tolerate the pastor just firing staff." When anxiety hits length of tenure does not matter much—in fact, it may become one more arrow in the opponent's quiver ("You've been here too long," "That staff person should have left five years ago." "We need new blood and fresh ideas."). This notion also assumes that length of tenure provides some "rights" and "privileges." That may be true in more formal organizations that recognize length of tenure as a value, but it's not universally true in congregations. (Andrew Bierce said that fidelity is "A virtue peculiar to those who are about to be betrayed.").¹ As to the issue of the pastor firing staff, that's one loaded with all sorts of angles. In some churches it may be that staff is expendable while the pastor is not. Or the congregation may hold to a "theology of hire" rather than a "theology of call" related to staff. In other words, an un-theological view that "the pastor hires staff" as opposed to the congregation, as a community of faith, *calls* its staff.

"I'm competent at what I do and I carry out my work responsibly." Aside from the fact that this is a given—you are *expected* to be good at your job—the fact of the matter is few congregational members will have any idea of what you do at your job and ministry. Program staff tend to be behind-the-scenes persons and their sphere of influence will tend to be small and focused, often by virtue of program areas: youth, children, adults, senior adults, educational programs, etc. Usually most people will not notice how good a job you are doing—but they'll immediately notice if you drop the ball on something!

"But I've gotten glowing personnel reports every year! How can they now say I'm not doing a good job?!" Sadly, most congregational personnel committees tend to be ineffective if not dysfunctional. Often these committees consist of people in the congregation who have no idea about what you do, may have only a passing personal acquaintance with you, and, tend to have no idea about how or why they are meeting for the annual personnel review with staff. Additionally, there tends to be a high turnover in these committees—no one wants to be critical of staff (except for the occasional willful persons who get on the committee to work out their issues with the church) and few church members feel competent enough to evaluate the specialized kind of ministries that second chairs carry out. Paradoxically, the more responsible members take the view that if they don't supervise you, why should they evaluate you?

When conflict spikes to a certain point, either because of circumstances or relationships, staff need to do the work of discernment about whether to stay or go. This is not easy and can be heartbreaking. But I've seen too many staff persons take a naive posture and just "hope for the best" or trust that persons will be reasonable and redemptive. Sadly, often that's just setting oneself up for a tragic surprise by putting one's fate in the hands of others. So, how do you know when to fold 'em? Here are some thoughts based on my observation of staff (second chair) terminations over the years:

- When you realize that you are working with a pastor who does not want you there (this is not an issue of fairness. A better question is, "Why would you want to stay in a place where you are not wanted?")
- When your job and ministry become oppressive rather than life-affirming

- When your family is suffering from the fallout of the toxicity from your job
- When the pastor gives you an ultimatum about "getting on board" with no room for dialogue or compromise
- When the pastor or a group in the church start to micromanage your ministry
- When you discern that you have become the scapegoat for misplaced anxiety and blaming
- When you cannot support the pastor's vision for the church
- When the pastor tells you that you're "not spiritual enough" or that "your commitment is lacking"
- When someone starts insisting on or counting office hours or insists that you need to "work harder"
- When staff is issued a "gag order" ("What happens in the church office stays in the church office.")
- When you are made responsible, and held accountable, for other people's functioning
- When the pastor, other staff, or church members begin to undermine your ministry and your effectiveness
- When you're called into the pastor's office for a "talk" and discover that representatives from the trustees and/or personnel are present (that's not a posture of "dialogue" — that's a power play intended to cover people's rear ends when a termination is coming)
- When neither the environment or working relationships contribute to your personal, spiritual, or, professional growth
- When there is no joy in what you do.

Lest this sound like a tirade against pastors and senior pastors let me say three things: (1) first, let's confess that sometimes, it *is* the pastor; but, (2) often it's a consequence of the challenge of pastoral leadership functioning in a complex and chronically anxious system. I don't think pastors intentionally want to function in unhealthy, unredemptive, reactive ways that are detrimental to self, others, and their congregations. But we should never underestimate the pressure of an anxious system on leaders who lack the resources to do self-care, self-work, or lack the capacity to function in self-differentiated ways. Never underestimate the power of systemic emotional process on the person on the end-point of anxiety (especially if it involves acute anxiety)—respect the power of homeostasis that facilitates a system to call out the leader who matches all of the system's neuroses; (3) accept that the relationship between pastor and staff is complex and fraught with difficulties. Trust, mutual respect, collegiality, and just working out a good working relationship takes time, commitment, vulnerability, honesty, mutual accountability, trust, and requires personal and spiritual maturity on the part of all players. How often do persons come together that can facilitate that constellation? How often do people give themselves enough time and opportunity to develop that kind of a relationship? The more common pattern in congregations seems to be that the pastor has little interest in meeting with and spending time with staff colleagues—despite all their talk of being a "team player" or "team leader." I don't think I'm being harsh here—take a poll among second chairs and see what response you get.

Here's the bottom line: the matter comes down to integrity of self. God will hold you more accountable for your response to your calling and ministry than God will others (and, by the way, that means *leaving well* regardless of the fairness of your treatment). Life is too short to allow ourselves to be caught in oppressive and unhealthy contexts and relationships. While there is no perfect congregation or place of ministry (and none populated by perfect Christians that I've been able to discover) there are places that are healthy, redemptive, affirming, and call out the best in people. None of us who are called of God, and who accept the call to ministry, are called to minister in places that are toxic to spirit, mind, or family—especially when fostered by those who claim to be disciples of Christ.

[1]Quoted in *The Routledge Dictionary of Quotations* (New York: Routlegue, 1987), p. 98.

Bibliography

Alexander, John B.; Groller, Richard and Morris Janet. *The Warrior's Edge: Frontline Strategies for Victory on the Corporate Battlefield.* New York: Avon Books, 1990.

Barbara Brown Taylor. *The Christian Century* (July 25, 2006): 31.

Boers·Arthur Paul *Never Call Them Jerks.* Herndon: The Alban Institute, 1999.

Bowen, Murray and Kerr, Michael. *Family Evaluation.,* New York: W. W. Norton & Co., 1988

Brueggemann, Walter., "The Preacher, The Text, and the People," *Theology Today* 47 (1990): 237-47.

Bullock, Richard and Bruesehoff, Richard J. *The Alban Guide to Sabbatical Planning.* Herndon: The Alban Institute, 2000.

Edwards, Betty. *Drawing on the Right Side of the Brain.* Los Angeles, California: J.P. Tarcher, 1989.

Friedman, Edwin H. *A Failure of Nerve.* New York: Seabury Books, 2007.

Galindo, Israel. *The Hidden Lives of Congregations.* Herndon: The Alban Institute, 2004.

_____; Boomer, Elaine; and Reagan, Don. *A Family Genogram Workbook.* Richmond: Educational Consultants, 2006.

Jinkins, Michael and Deborah. "Surviving Frustration in the First Years," *Congregations,* Jan/Feb 1994.

Mann, Alice. *The In-Between Church: Navigating Size Transitions in Congregations.* Herndon: The Alban Institute, 1998.

Marcuson, Margaret. *Leaders Who Last.* New York: Seabury Books, 2009.

McIntosh, Gary L. *One Size Doesn't Fit All: Bringing Out the Best in Any Size Church.* New York: Fleming H Revell Co., 1999.

Richardson, Ronald. *Creating a Healthier Church.* New York: Fortress Press, 1996.